HMH SCIENCE DIMENSIONS™
GEOLOGIC PROCESSES & HISTORY

Module F

This Write-In Book belongs to

_____

Teacher/Room

_____

Houghton Mifflin Harcourt™

Consulting Authors

Michael A. DiSpezio

Global Educator
North Falmouth, Massachusetts

Michael DiSpezio has authored many HMH instructional programs for Science and Mathematics. He has also authored numerous trade books and multimedia programs on various topics and hosted dozens of studio and location broadcasts for various organizations in the U.S. and worldwide. Most recently, he has been working with educators to provide strategies for implementing the Next Generation Science Standards, particularly the science and engineering practices, cross-cutting concepts, and the use of Evidence Notebooks. To all his projects, he brings his extensive background in science, his expertise in classroom teaching at the elementary, middle, and high school levels, and his deep experience in producing interactive and engaging instructional materials.

Marjorie Frank

Science Writer and Content-Area Reading Specialist
Brooklyn, New York

An educator and linguist by training, a writer and poet by nature, Marjorie Frank has authored and designed a generation of instructional materials in all subject areas, including past HMH Science programs. Her other credits include authoring science issues of an award-winning children's magazine, writing game-based digital assessments, developing blended learning materials for young children, and serving as instructional designer and co-author of pioneering school-to-work software. In addition, she has served on the adjunct faculty of Hunter, Manhattan, and Brooklyn Colleges, teaching courses in science methods, literacy, and writing. For *HMH Science Dimensions™*, she has guided the development of our K–2 strands and our approach to making connections between NGSS and Common Core ELA/literacy standards.

Acknowledgments

Cover credits: (prehistoric fly caught in amber) ©PjrStudio/Alamy; (geode with hammer) ©Houghton Mifflin Harcourt.

Section Header Master Art: (rivers on top of Greenland ice sheet) ©Maria-José Viñas, NASA Earth Science News Team

Copyright © 2018 by Houghton Mifflin Harcourt Publishing Company

Printed in the U.S.A.

ISBN   978-0-544-86099-5

4 5 6 7 8 9 10   0877   25 24 23 22 21 20 19 18 17

4500645473   A B C D E F G

Michael R. Heithaus, Ph.D.

Dean, College Of Arts, Sciences & Education Professor, Department Of Biological Sciences
Florida International University
Miami, Florida

Mike Heithaus joined the FIU Biology Department in 2003, has served as Director of the Marine Sciences Program and Executive Director of the School of Environment, Arts, and Society, which brings together the natural and social sciences and humanities to develop solutions to today's environmental challenges. He now serves as Dean of the College of Arts, Sciences & Education. His research focuses on predator-prey interactions and the ecological importance of large marine species. He has helped to guide the development of Life Science content in *HMH Science Dimensions™*, with a focus on strategies for teaching challenging content as well as the science and engineering practices of analyzing data and using computational thinking.

Cary I. Sneider, Ph.D.

Associate Research Professor Portland State University Portland, Oregon

While studying astrophysics at Harvard, Cary Sneider volunteered to teach in an Upward Bound program and discovered his real calling as a science teacher. After teaching middle and high school science in Maine, California, Costa Rica and Micronesia, he settled for nearly three decades at Lawrence Hall of Science in Berkeley, California, where he developed skills in curriculum development and teacher education. Over his career Cary directed more than 20 federal, state, and foundation grant projects, and was a writing team leader for the Next Generation Science Standards. He has been instrumental in ensuring *HMH Science Dimensions™* meets the high expectations of the NGSS and provides an effective three-dimensional learning experience for all students.

Program Advisors

Paul D. Asimow
Eleanor and John R. McMillan Professor of Geology and Geochemistry
California Institute of Technology
Pasadena, California

Dr. Eileen Cashman
Professor
Humboldt State University
Arcata, California

Elizabeth A. De Stasio
Raymond J. Herzog Professor of Science
Lawrence University
Appleton, Wisconsin

Perry Donham
Lecturer
Boston University
Boston, Massachusetts

Shila Garg, Ph.D.
Emerita Professor of Physics Former Dean of Faculty & Provost
The College of Wooster
Wooster, Ohio

Tatiana A. Krivosheev
Professor of Physics
Clayton State University
Morrow, Georgia

Mark B. Moldwin
Professor of Space Sciences and Engineering
University of Michigan
Ann Arbor, Michigan

Kelly Y. Neiles, Ph.D.
Assistant Professor of Chemistry
St. Mary's College of Maryland
St. Mary's City, Maryland

Dr. Sten Odenwald
Astronomer
NASA Goddard Spaceflight Center
Greenbelt, Maryland

Bruce W. Schafer
Executive Director
Oregon Robotics Tournament & Outreach Program
Beaverton, Oregon

Barry A. Van Deman
President and CEO
Museum of Life and Science
Durham, North Carolina

Kim Withers, Ph.D.
Assistant Professor
Texas A&M University-Corpus Christi
Corpus Christi, Texas

Adam D. Woods, Ph.D.
Professor
California State University, Fullerton
Fullerton, California

Classroom Reviewers

Cynthia Book, Ph.D.
John Barrett Middle School
Carmichael, California

Katherine Carter, M.Ed.
Fremont Unified School District
Fremont, California

Theresa Hollenbeck, M.Ed.
Winston Churchill Middle School
Carmichael, California

Kathryn S. King
Science and AVID Teacher
Norwood Jr. High School
Sacramento, California

Donna Lee
Science/STEM Teacher
Junction Ave. K8
Livermore, California

Rebecca S. Lewis
Science Teacher
North Rockford Middle School
Rockford, Michigan

Bryce McCourt
*8th Grade Science Teacher/Middle
School Curriculum Chair*
Cudahy Middle School
Cudahy, Wisconsin

Sarah Mrozinski
Teacher
St. Sebastian School
Milwaukee, Wisconsin

Raymond Pietersen
Science Program Specialist
Elk Grove Unified School District
Elk Grove, California

**Richard M. Stec, M.A.–
Curriculum, Instruction, and
Supervision**
District Science Supervisor
West Windsor-Plainsboro
Regional School District
West Windsor, New Jersey

Anne Vitale
STEM Supervisor
Randolph Middle School
Randolph, New Jersey

You are a scientist!
You are naturally curious.

Have you ever wondered . . .

- why is it difficult to catch a fly?
- how a new island can appear in an ocean?
- how to design a great tree house?
- how a spacecraft can send messages across the solar system?

HMH SCIENCE DIMENSIONS™

will *SPARK* your curiosity!

AND prepare you for

✓	tomorrow
✓	next year
✓	college or career
✓	life!

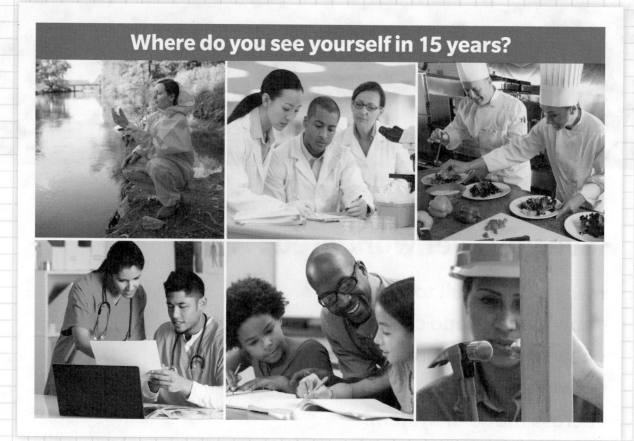

Where do you see yourself in 15 years?

Observe

Collect Data

Be a scientist.
Work like real scientists work.

Analyze

Be an engineer.

Solve problems like engineers do.

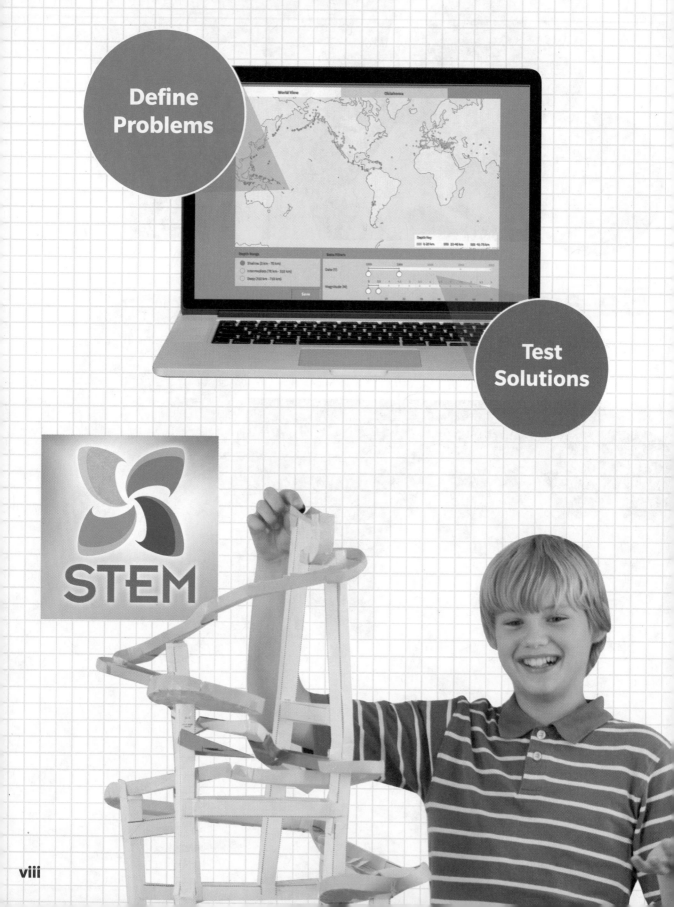

Define Problems

Test Solutions

STEM

Gather Information

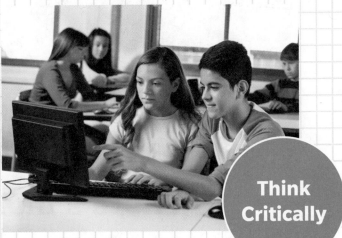

Think Critically

Explain your world.

Start by asking questions.

Conduct Investigations

Collaborate

Develop Explanations

Construct Arguments

There's more than one way to the answer. What's YOURS?

YOUR Program

Write-In Book:

- a brand-new and innovative textbook that will guide you through your next generation curriculum, including your hands-on lab program

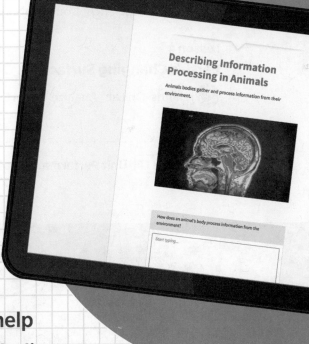

Interactive Online Student Edition:

- a complete online version of your textbook enriched with videos, interactivities, animations, simulations, and room to enter data, draw, and store your work

More tools are available online to help you practice and learn science, including:

- **Hands-On Labs**
- **Science and Engineering Practices Handbook**
- **Crosscutting Concepts Handbook**
- **English Language Arts Handbook**
- **Math Handbook**

UNIT 1

The Dynamic Earth

Lesson 1
Weathering, Erosion, and Deposition 4

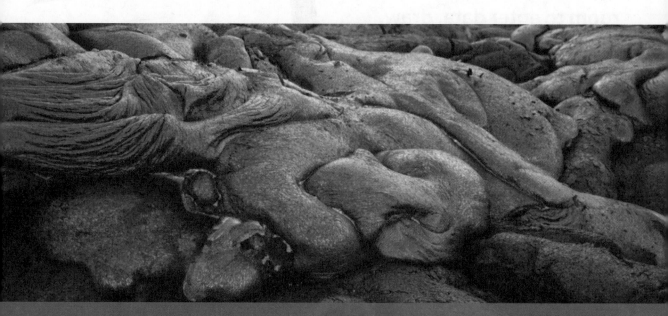 Hands-On Lab Model Erosion and Deposition 15

Lesson 2
The Rock Cycle 22

Hands-On Lab Model Crystal Formation 27

Lesson 3
Earth's Plates 46

Hands-On Lab Model the Movement of Continents 58

People in Science Doug Gibbons, Research Scientist Assistant 63

Lesson 4
Earth's Changing Surface 68

Hands-On Lab Analyze Visual Evidence 78

Unit Review 87

ENGINEER IT Unit Performance Task 91

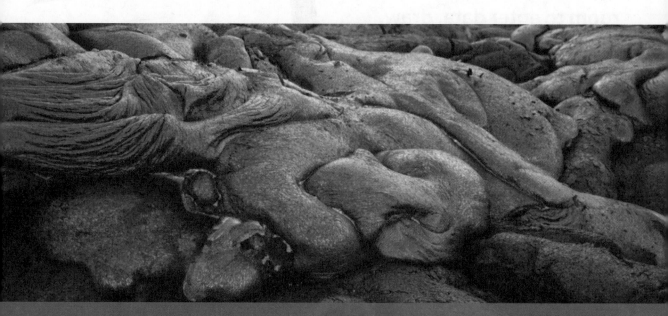
Lava flows often cool quickly, hardening into rock.

UNIT 2   93

Earth Through Time

Lesson 1
The Age of Earth's Rocks 96

 Hands-On Lab Model Rock Layers to Determine Relative Age 102

Lesson 2
Earth's History 114

 Hands-On Lab Construct a Timeline 123

Careers in Science Paleoartist 127

Unit Review 133

ENGINEER IT Unit Performance Task 137

Starfish can become buried by sediment. Over time, the sediment hardens into rock, preserving the starfish as a fossil.

Whether you are in the lab or in the field, you are responsible for your own safety and the safety of others. To fulfill these responsibilities and avoid accidents, be aware of the safety of your classmates as well as your own safety at all times. Take your lab work and field work seriously, and behave appropriately. Elements of safety to keep in mind are shown below and on the following pages.

Safety in the Lab

- [ ] Be sure you understand the materials, your procedure, and the safety rules before you start an investigation in the lab.

- [ ] Know where to find and how to use fire extinguishers, eyewash stations, shower stations, and emergency power shut-offs.

- [ ] Use proper safety equipment. Always wear personal protective equipment, such as eye protection and gloves, when setting up labs, during labs, and when cleaning up.

- [ ] Do not begin until your teacher has told you to start. Follow directions.

- [ ] Keep the lab neat and uncluttered. Clean up when you are finished. Report all spills to your teacher immediately. Watch for slip/fall and trip/fall hazards.

- [ ] If you or another student are injured in any way, tell your teacher immediately, even if the injury seems minor.

- [ ] Do not take any food or drink into the lab. Never take any chemicals out of the lab.

Safety in the Field

- [ ] Be sure you understand the goal of your fieldwork and the proper way to carry out the investigation before you begin fieldwork.

- [ ] Use proper safety equipment and personal protective equipment, such as eye protection, that suits the terrain and the weather.

- [ ] Follow directions, including appropriate safety procedures as provided by your teacher.

- [ ] Do not approach or touch wild animals. Do not touch plants unless instructed by your teacher to do so. Leave natural areas as you found them.

- [ ] Stay with your group.

- [ ] Use proper accident procedures, and let your teacher know about a hazard in the environment or an accident immediately, even if the hazard or accident seems minor.

Safety Symbols

To highlight specific types of precautions, the following symbols are used throughout the lab program. Remember that no matter what safety symbols you see within each lab, all safety rules should be followed at all times.

Dress Code

- Wear safety goggles (or safety glasses as appropriate for the activity) at all times in the lab as directed. If chemicals get into your eye, flush your eyes immediately for a minimum of 15 minutes.
- Do not wear contact lenses in the lab.
- Do not look directly at the sun or any intense light source or laser.
- Wear appropriate protective non-latex gloves as directed.
- Wear an apron or lab coat at all times in the lab as directed.
- Tie back long hair, secure loose clothing, and remove loose jewelry. Remove acrylic nails when working with active flames.
- Do not wear open-toed shoes, sandals, or canvas shoes in the lab.

Glassware and Sharp Object Safety

- Do not use chipped or cracked glassware.
- Use heat-resistant glassware for heating or storing hot materials.
- Notify your teacher immediately if a piece of glass breaks.
- Use extreme care when handling any sharp and pointed instruments.
- Do not cut an object while holding the object unsupported in your hands. Place the object on a suitable cutting surface, and always cut in a direction away from your body.

Chemical Safety

- If a chemical gets on your skin, on your clothing, or in your eyes, rinse it immediately for a minimum of 15 minutes (using the shower, faucet, or eyewash station), and alert your teacher.
- Do not clean up spilled chemicals unless your teacher directs you to do so.
- Do not inhale any gas or vapor unless directed to do so by your teacher. If you are instructed to note the odor of a substance, wave the fumes toward your nose with your hand. This is called wafting. Never put your nose close to the source of the odor.
- Handle materials that emit vapors or gases in a well-ventilated area.
- Keep your hands away from your face while you are working on any activity.

Safety Symbols, continued

Electrical Safety

- Do not use equipment with frayed electrical cords or loose plugs.
- Do not use electrical equipment near water or when clothing or hands are wet.
- Hold the plug housing when you plug in or unplug equipment. Do not pull on the cord.
- Use only GFI protected electrical receptacles.

Heating and Fire Safety

- Be aware of any source of flames, sparks, or heat (such as flames, heating coils, or hot plates) before working with any flammable substances.
- Know the location of lab fire extinguisher and fire-safety blankets.
- Know your school's fire-evacuation routes.
- If your clothing catches on fire, walk to the lab shower to put out the fire. Do not run.
- Never leave a hot plate unattended while it is turned on or while it is cooling.
- Use tongs or appropriate insulated holders when handling heated objects.
- Allow all equipment to cool before storing it.

Plant and Animal Safety

- Do not eat any part of a plant.
- Do not pick any wild plant unless your teacher instructs you to do so.
- Handle animals only as your teacher directs.
- Treat animals carefully and respectfully.
- Wash your hands throughly with soap and water after handling any plant or animal.

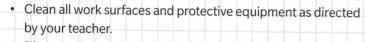

Cleanup

- Clean all work surfaces and protective equipment as directed by your teacher.
- Dispose of hazardous materials or sharp objects only as directed by your teacher.
- Wash your hands throughly with soap and water before you leave the lab or after any activity.

Student Safety Quiz

Circle the letter of the BEST answer.

1. Before starting an investigation or lab procedure, you should
   A. try an experiment of your own
   B. open all containers and packages
   C. read all directions and make sure you understand them
   D. handle all the equipment to become familiar with it

2. At the end of any activity you should
   A. wash your hands thoroughly with soap and water before leaving the lab
   B. cover your face with your hands
   C. put on your safety goggles
   D. leave hot plates switched on

3. If you get hurt or injured in any way, you should
   A. tell your teacher immediately
   B. find bandages or a first aid kit
   C. go to your principal's office
   D. get help after you finish the lab

4. If your glassware is chipped or broken, you should
   A. use it only for solid materials
   B. give it to your teacher for recycling or disposal
   C. put it back into the storage cabinet
   D. increase the damage so that it is obvious

5. If you have unused chemicals after finishing a procedure, you should
   A. pour them down a sink or drain
   B. mix them all together in a bucket
   C. put them back into their original containers
   D. dispose of them as directed by your teacher

6. If electrical equipment has a frayed cord, you should
   A. unplug the equipment by pulling the cord
   B. let the cord hang over the side of a counter or table
   C. tell your teacher about the problem immediately
   D. wrap tape around the cord to repair it

7. If you need to determine the odor of a chemical or a solution, you should
   A. use your hand to bring fumes from the container to your nose
   B. bring the container under your nose and inhale deeply
   C. tell your teacher immediately
   D. use odor-sensing equipment

8. When working with materials that might fly into the air and hurt someone's eye, you should wear
   A. goggles
   B. an apron
   C. gloves
   D. a hat

9. Before doing experiments involving a heat source, you should know the location of the
   A. door
   B. window
   C. fire extinguisher
   D. overhead lights

10. If you get chemicals in your eye you should
    A. wash your hands immediately
    B. put the lid back on the chemical container
    C. wait to see if your eye becomes irritated
    D. use the eyewash station right away, for a minimum of 15 minutes

Go online to view the Lab Safety Handbook for additional information.

The Dynamic Earth

Lesson 1 Weathering, Erosion, and Deposition 4

Lesson 2 The Rock Cycle 22

Lesson 3 Earth's Plates 46

Lesson 4 Earth's Changing Surface 68

Unit Review 87

Unit Performance Task 91

Six million years ago, Earth's surface in the area now known as the Grand Canyon was flat. The Colorado River cut down into the rock and formed the Grand Canyon over millions of years.

Many of Earth's scenic and interesting geologic features seem to be constant, as if they were always there. Mountains, canyons, caves, plains, and other formations are mostly unchanged during the course of a human lifetime. Sometimes an earthquake will shake the ground, a volcano will erupt, or a sudden flood will wash away coastline. Scientists study these events and patterns to explain the processes that change Earth's surface. In this unit, you will investigate the processes that make Earth's surface such a dynamic and beautiful place.

Why It Matters

Here are some questions to consider as you work through the unit. Can you answer any of the questions now? Revisit these questions at the end of the unit to apply what you discover.

Questions	Notes
What are some geologic features near where you live?	
How do these features affect the people who live there?	
What changes have you seen in the geology of your area?	
What causes those changes?	
How can human activity speed up or slow down the changes?	
What are the benefits or risks associated with these changes?	

Unit Starter: Identifying Geologic Features

A geologic feature, such as a mountain or a river, is the result of the geologic processes that have occurred on Earth. This map of San Francisco shows geologic features and other features such as streets and manmade landmarks.

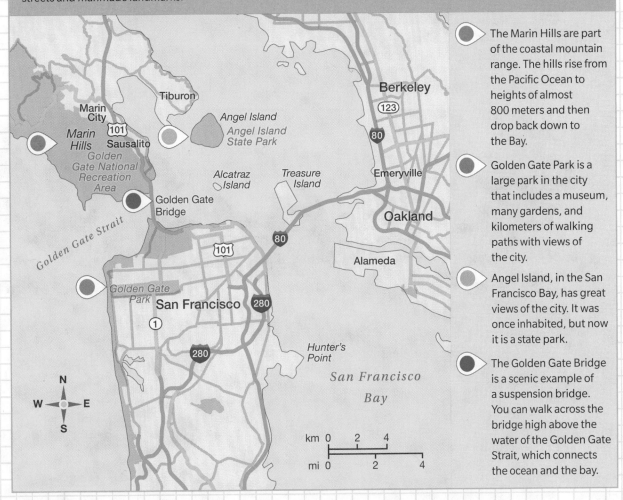

The Marin Hills are part of the coastal mountain range. The hills rise from the Pacific Ocean to heights of almost 800 meters and then drop back down to the Bay.

Golden Gate Park is a large park in the city that includes a museum, many gardens, and kilometers of walking paths with views of the city.

Angel Island, in the San Francisco Bay, has great views of the city. It was once inhabited, but now it is a state park.

The Golden Gate Bridge is a scenic example of a suspension bridge. You can walk across the bridge high above the water of the Golden Gate Strait, which connects the ocean and the bay.

1. Which of the following are geologic features on the map? Select all that apply.

   A. Angel Island
   B. Golden Gate Bridge
   C. Golden Gate Park
   D. Marin Hills

Go online to download the Unit Project Worksheet to help you plan your project.

Unit Project

Feature Future

Can you predict the future of a geologic feature? Choose a geologic feature near where you live or one in another location that interests you. Then use evidence to make inferences about its past, investigate present conditions, and predict its future!

Weathering, Erosion, and Deposition

The rock structures on Praia do Camilo in Lagos, Algarve region, Portugal have formed over many years.

By the end of this lesson . . .

you will have investigated how the processes of weathering, erosion, and deposition have shaped Earth's surface.

Go online to view the digital version of the Hands-On Lab for this lesson and to download additional lab resources.

CAN YOU EXPLAIN IT?

What caused these changes at Port Campbell National Park?

before 1990

after 1990

The photo on the left shows a rock formation just offshore of Port Campbell National Park in Australia before 1990. The photo on the right shows the same rock formation after 1990.

The Earth's surface can change in the blink of an eye, or so it seems. While some events can appear to happen quickly, it may have taken many years to build up to that point. As you look at the photographs of the rock formation in Port Campbell National Park, evidence of change appears obvious, but the story may be more complex.

1. What types of changes do you observe between the rock formations in the two images?

2. Based on the visible changes in the rock formation, do you think the changes occurred quickly or slowly over time? Explain your reasoning.

 EVIDENCE NOTEBOOK As you explore the lesson, gather evidence that will explain what happened to the rock formation in Australia over time.

Identifying Effects of Weathering

Rocks and other materials that make up Earth's surface are matter. So, rock and other materials cannot be created or destroyed. But they can be changed. **Weathering** is the process by which rock materials are broken down by the action of physical and chemical processes.

Weathering changes rocks by breaking them into smaller and smaller pieces, or by dissolving the rock. Fragments of weathered rock, called **sediment,** are an important part of soil. Sediment can build up in layers on Earth's surface and create rock formations, sand dunes, and other features.

When it comes to weathering, not all rocks are created equal. Some rocks, such as granite, are made of minerals that are more resistant to weathering than other rocks. Surface area also affects a rock's tendency to weather. A large block of rock will weather more slowly than smaller broken pieces of the same rock. This difference is because the smaller pieces have more surface area exposed to agents of physical and chemical weathering. Physical and chemical weathering are the two main types of weathering that you'll explore next.

Look closely at the shape of this rock formation in South Coyote Buttes Wilderness in Arizona.

3. Many features found in South Coyote Buttes have this same striking appearance. What could cause rocks to be shaped this way? Explain your answer.

Physical Weathering

Physical weathering is the mechanical breakdown of rocks into smaller pieces. Physical weathering involves only physical changes. Rocks can be physically weathered by temperature changes, pressure changes, and interactions with plants, animals, water, wind, ice, and the force of gravity.

Types of Physical Weathering

Water can seep into tiny cracks in rocks and then freeze. Water expands when it freezes, causing the cracks in the rocks to widen. Cycles of repeated freezing and thawing eventually fracture the rock.

Plant roots can grow into gaps in rocks. Over time, as the roots grow, they force the gaps wider, causing the rock to break apart.

Abrasion occurs when rock is reduced in size by the scraping action of other rock materials. Abrasion is driven by water, wind, ice, or gravity. A strong wind, for example, can blow sediments against rock surfaces, wearing down the rock. Abrasion can make angular rocks smooth and rounded.

4. Which statements describe physical weathering? Select all that apply.

   A. Two rocks hit against each other in a fast-flowing stream and break apart.

   B. Oxygen and water react with certain minerals in a rock, dissolving the minerals.

   C. Small rocks are tossed together when a mole digs an underground den.

   D. Mosses grow on a rock and produce acids that wear away the rock over time.

Plants are not the only living things that can cause physical weathering. Animals physically weather rocks in a variety of ways. Burrowing animals dig in soil and expose or displace rocks. Even strolling along a well-worn path in a meadow exposes buried rocks to wind, water, air, and other agents of weathering.

Chemical Weathering

Chemical weathering is the chemical breakdown and decomposition of rocks by natural processes. Unlike physical weathering, chemical weathering changes the appearance of rocks through a chemical process. It weakens or dissolves rock over time. Agents of chemical weathering include air, water, and plants. For example, groundwater, which is water found below Earth's surface, can contain natural acids that dissolve rocks. Underground caves form in this way.

Types of Chemical Weathering

 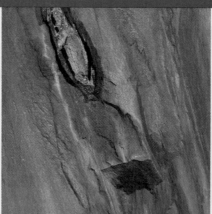 

Acid precipitation is rain or other precipitation that is more acidic than normal. Acid precipitation reacts with certain types of rocks, weakening them and making them more susceptible to physical weathering. The rocks break down over time.

Iron-containing rocks can react with oxygen and water in a process called oxidation. Oxidation can give the rocks a reddish color, similar to rust. In fact, the same process causes rust to form on bicycles left out in the rain.

Plants such as lichens and mosses produce weak acids. When the plants grow on rocks, the acids slowly, but steadily, wear down the rocks.

5. Which description is evidence of chemical weathering?

    A. A rock in a windy desert has scratches on its surface.

    B. A rock in a tundra has deep cracks filled with ice.

    C. A rock turns a reddish color when exposed to air and water.

    D. A rock on a steep slope falls to the ground and breaks apart.

Earlier, you learned that the surface area and composition of a rock affect its rate of weathering. Other factors that affect rates of weathering include location and climate. Rocks on steep slopes are more likely to be displaced by gravity and exposed to wind, water, and air. Rocks in cold climates are more likely to experience physical weathering caused by cycles of freezing and thawing. In contrast, chemical weathering occurs more rapidly in warm, wet climates because warm temperatures increase rates of chemical processes. Both types of weathering tend to happen more slowly in dry climates.

 EVIDENCE NOTEBOOK

    6. Does the collapsed rock formation in Australia show signs of weathering? If so, identify the type of weathering that could have occurred. Record your evidence.

7. Language SmArts | Find Evidence for Weathering Analyze each photo and identify the correct terms to complete each statement. Then provide evidence to support your answer choices.

Weathering Example	Weathering Type or Agent	Evidence
	This rock is an example of chemical / physical weathering as a result of acid / wind / ice.	
	This rock is an example of chemical / physical weathering as a result of acid / wind / ice.	
	This rock is an example of chemical / physical weathering as a result of acid / wind / ice.	

Analyze the Effects of Weathering

Weathering is an important process that changes Earth's surface. These changes happen on different scales of time and space. A rock tumbles to the ground and breaks apart—this is a fast change that affects a small area. Water and wind steadily wear down a mountain over millions of years—this is a slow change that affects a large area.

8. Discuss With a partner, look at the stone bricks used to build this building and think about how they changed over time. What caused them to change? Do you think these changes occurred quickly or slowly? Explain.

_____

_____

_____

_____

Lesson 1 Weathering, Erosion, and Deposition **9**

Exploring Agents of Erosion and Deposition

Picture a fast-flowing stream. Rocks tumble together, breaking up into sediment that is carried away and dropped in a new place. Some of the rock material dissolves in the water and is carried downstream. **Erosion** is the process by which wind, water, ice, or gravity transport weathered materials from one location to another. **Deposition** occurs when the eroded materials are laid down. Erosion and deposition, like weathering, do not destroy matter. Instead, they move and deposit matter in new places.

Wind and Water

Recall that wind and water can cause weathering through abrasion. Wind and water are also agents of erosion and deposition. Water erodes as it flows above ground through streams or underground through spaces in rock. Wind erodes as it blows over surfaces and picks up sediments. When wind and water lose energy and slow down, they drop their sediments and deposition occurs.

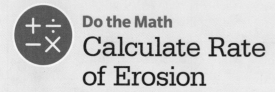

Do the Math

Calculate Rate of Erosion

The environment, very much like an equation, is balanced. Since matter is not destroyed by natural processes, it can only move and cycle through Earth's subsystems. As erosion occurs it takes away from, or subtracts, sediment from one location and deposits, or adds, it to another location.

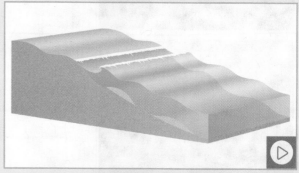

As sand erodes from a beach, it can be deposited into sand bars.

9. Identify the correct type of change that occurs.

    A. Erosion, by definition, represents a(n) *increase / decrease* in height.

    B. Deposition represents a(n) *increase / decrease* in height.

    C. As sand is eroded by waves and deposited on the sand bar, the sand bar *increases / decreases* in height.

10. During a storm, sand is eroded from a beach at a rate of 2 m³ per hour. What equation can be used to represent the volume of sand in cubic meters, c, on the beach? Let b represent the amount of sand in cubic meters at the beginning of the storm and h represent time in hours. Complete the equation using +, −, ×, or ÷.

    $c = b$ ☐ $2h$

11. Suppose the total volume of sand on the beach is 1,278 m³. What will its volume be after 24 hours of erosion?

Erosion and Deposition by Wind and Water

How will water and wind shape the land in each of these areas?

Waves constantly crash against the shoreline, eroding this rocky coast. Waves also erode sediments from sandy beaches.

Over millions of years, a river can carve a rugged valley through the processes of weathering and erosion.

This rock formation has been shaped by wind abrasion, a type of weathering. Wind erosion then transported the weathered sediments to a new place.

A river slows down when it reaches the ocean. There is no longer enough energy to carry sediments, and they are deposited at the mouth of the river to form a feature called a delta. When a river floods, the shape of the delta can quickly change.

Sand dunes form when wind deposits its load of sediments. Sand dune patterns are constantly changing due to erosion and deposition. Patterns can shift in time scales that range from hours to years.

12. **Discuss** A friend looks at these images and says that sand and sediment are being destroyed during the process of erosion. Form into small groups and discuss whether you think the friend is correct. Use evidence to support your response.

Ice

One of the most powerful agents of erosion and deposition is ice. A glacier is a large mass of ice that exists year-round and flows slowly over land. The weight of the glacier, along with gravity, help it move over land. As glaciers move, they act like a conveyor belt, eroding soil, sediment, and rock—even large boulders—over great distances, and then depositing the materials elsewhere. Glaciers can form jagged peaks or flatten and scoop out large sections of land creating valleys. The Great Lakes are huge depressions formed by glaciers and later filled in with water. Glacial deposits can create long winding ridges or rocky mounds of sediment.

This cutaway view of a glacier reveals the sediment and rocks that can be picked up, carried, and deposited by the glacier as it flows across the surface of the Earth.

13. How will the glacier affect surrounding land as it moves and melts over time?

Gravity

Energy from the sun powers the movement of wind and water. But the force of gravity, which attracts matter to Earth's center, also plays a role in driving these agents of erosion. When wind slows down, its load of sediment drops to the ground because of gravity. Rocks, boulders, and soil fall down slopes because of gravity. Water flows downhill, through valleys and waterfalls, because of gravity. Gravity is the main force behind sudden rock falls and landslides that can change the shape of a mountain.

landslide

waterfall

14. Explain the role of gravity in the landslide and in the waterfall.

15. Look at the image of the rock ledge. What factors could contribute to a collapse of the ledge? Select all that apply.

   A. Wind

   B. Water

   C. Ice

   D. Gravity

16. Explain how each of the contributing factors would play a role in the collapse of the ledge.

Found near the coast of Palau, Italy, this rock formation shows evidence of weathering.

 EVIDENCE NOTEBOOK

   17. Will gravity always play a role in erosion of a shoreline feature, such as the collapse of a rock formation in Australia? If so, identify the process, or processes, that would lead up to the collapse. Record your evidence.

Identify Areas of Erosion and Deposition

Weathering, erosion, and deposition are geologic processes that are mostly powered by energy from the sun. These changes happen on different scales of time and space. Yet each change can be studied to help predict how Earth will change in the future.

18. On the map, label the areas where erosion occurs with an E and then label the areas where deposition occurs with a D. Some areas may have both.

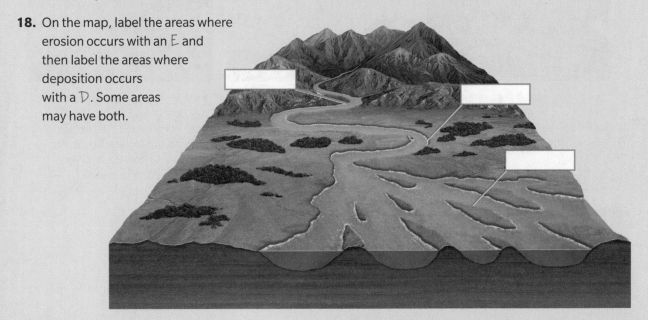

Modeling Weathering, Erosion, and Deposition

You can't re-create an actual flood in a lab, but you can use models to investigate the processes of weathering, erosion, and deposition. Computer simulations can also be used as models that can help you learn about past events and predict future ones. Computer models can be used to re-create events that cannot be studied directly, such as a massive flood in prehistoric times.

Studying a Historic Flood

The Missoula Floods were part of a historic event that took place over 10,000 years ago. These floods stretched across a large portion of the northwestern United States, leaving visible evidence of their path. In the early 1920s, scientists began to study this historic flood and the research continues today.

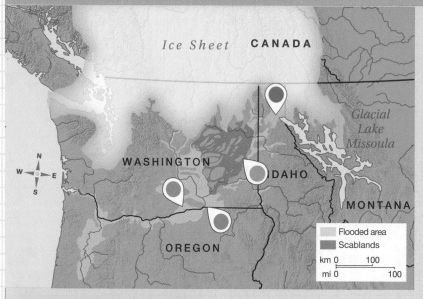

The map and these images model a massive flood that happened in the blink of a geologic eye. Keep in mind, though, that the processes of weathering and erosion worked on the ice dam for a long time before it finally broke.

During the last Ice Age, a huge ice dam held back Glacial Lake Missoula, a large body of water in western Montana. On multiple occasions, the dam burst. Water roared out, emptying the lake in just a few days.

Erosion caused by the roaring water carved out a landscape of huge waterfalls, deep canyons, and the towering ripple marks shown here.

When the rushing floodwaters reached narrow Wallula Gap, they would back up and halt for several days, forming a temporary lake some 240 m deep.

The Scablands cover at least 5,000 km² of land affected by the ancient floodwaters. The ice dam reformed and broke several times. During each flood, the land was scoured and stripped anew.

19. Engineer It What technology since the beginning of the space age makes it possible for us to understand the scale of changes that occurred as a result of the breaking of the glacial dam holding back Lake Missoula's waters so many years ago?

Hands-On Lab
Model Erosion and Deposition

How can you predict the effects of erosion and deposition? You will model Earth's surface with sand and then investigate the effects of erosion and deposition by water and wind.

MATERIALS
- two flat trays
- soil
- sand
- container of water
- colander with small holes

Procedure and Analysis

STEP 1 Make a mound of soil on a tray to represent a hill and a mound of sand on the other tray to represent a dune.

STEP 2 Predict what will happen to the features after a heavy storm. Record all your predictions and observations in the spaces provided.

STEP 3 Blow on the sand dune to simulate a coastal storm. Observe what happens.

STEP 4 Pour water through the colander and onto the hill, simulating rain. Observe what happens.

STEP 5 Pour water around the base of the dune. Carefully tilt the tray to model wave action. Observe what happens to the dune.

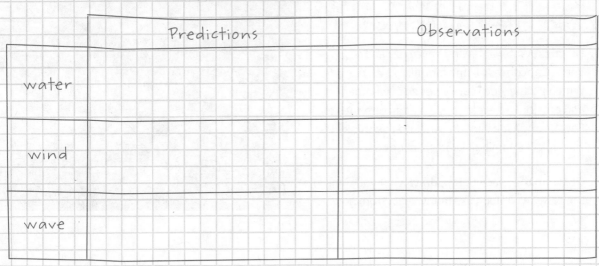

	Predictions	Observations
water		
wind		
wave		

STEP 6 Describe overall patterns of weathering, erosion, and deposition.

STEP 7 How can you use what you've learned about erosion in this activity?

Scales of Weathering, Erosion, and Deposition

Weathering, erosion, and deposition can happen over a wide range of time scales. Wind can change the shape of a sand dune in minutes. The erosion that forms a canyon can take place over millions of years. The size of the changes caused by weathering, erosion, and deposition can vary too. Some changes, such as acids weathering a rock, affect Earth's surface on a small, localized scale. Changes such as the formation of an ice sheet can affect a whole continent. By studying these processes, you can reconstruct past geologic events, such as the massive flood that occurred in the northwestern United States over 10,000 years ago. You can also make predictions about future events.

The Great Sphinx of Giza, Egypt.

20. The Sphinx in Egypt was likely built about 4,500 years ago. If weathering and erosion continue to have the same effect on the Sphinx, what do you think it will look like in 4,500 more years?

   A. It will not change.

   B. It will look more defined.

   C. It will look much less defined.

   D. It will disappear completely.

Predict Effects of Erosion

21. Discuss Water and wind have shaped Mesa Verde Canyon in Arizona for millions of years. With a partner, look for evidence of weathering and erosion in the canyon. If water continues to flow through the canyon, what do you think it will look like 1 million years from now?

22. Draw In the space below, draw what you think the canyon will look like many years from now.

Continue Your Exploration

Name: _____   Date: _____

Check out the path below or go online to choose one of the other paths shown.

| Gold Rush | • **Hands-On Labs** ✋
• **Sailing Stones**
• **Propose Your Own Path** | *Go online to choose one of these other paths.* |

Did you ever wonder why gold prospectors are often shown knee-deep in a shallow stream, panning for gold? Why do they look there?

The prospectors know that gold is subject to the natural processes of weathering, erosion, and deposition. This rare and beautiful mineral can be found in certain buried rocks. Gold is often found in veins, which are narrow zones within rock that contain minerals different from the rest of the rock. Weathering can expose these veins, wearing away nuggets or flakes of gold. Erosion carries the gold into streambeds. Deposition drops it in places where the stream flow slows down, such as near pools or sandbars.

When looking for gold in a stream, pans are used to sift through sediment and rocks.

Continue Your Exploration

Use your knowledge of erosion and deposition to answer the questions.

1. Suppose you inherit this model drawing of a piece of land your family owns. You decide you want to use the model to decide where to pan for gold. Identify four potential areas of erosion or deposition. Label the model with E or D to represent the areas of erosion (*E*) or deposition (*D*).

2. Describe what is happening in the areas of erosion and deposition.

3. In which area(s) would you search for gold? Explain.

4. **Collaborate** Discuss with a classmate where you would search. Did you identify the same places? Together, decide on which location you would search first and argue from evidence to support your decision.

Can You Explain It?

Name: _____   Date: _____

Revisit the changes to the rock formation on Australia's coastline.

What caused these changes at Port Campbell National Park?

EVIDENCE NOTEBOOK
Refer to the notes in your Evidence Notebook to help you construct an explanation of the causes of the changes at Port Campbell National Park.

1. State your claim. Make sure your claim fully explains how the changes at Port Campbell National Park occurred and provides evidence to support it.

2. Explain your reasoning. How does your evidence connect to and support your claim?

Checkpoints

Use the photo to answer questions 3–4.

3. For which of the following can you find evidence in this photo? Choose all that apply.

    A. erosion

    B. deposition

    C. chemical weathering

    D. physical weathering

4. Which processes could be primarily responsible for the formation of the alluvial fan shown in the photo?

    A. Wind storms coming through the base of the mountains into the valley

    B. Water flowing down from the mountains and depositing sediment at the base

    C. Rocks and boulders falling down the mountains and piling up at the base

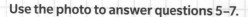

alluvial fan

Use the photo to answer questions 5–7.

5. Which of the following is a factor in weathering caused by gravity?

    A. presence of living organisms on the rocks

    B. presence of water at one end of the glacier

    C. slope of the glacier and surrounding area

    D. size of the boulders at the base of the glacier

6. Which evidence in the picture best illustrates the occurrence of deposition?

    A. the glacier ending in the water

    B. striations in the rock formations

    C. areas of water where the glacier may be melting

    D. dirt and various sizes of rocks at the base of the rock formations

7. What type of physical weathering causes the striations in the rock's surface?

    A. abrasion of the surface caused by rocks being moved under the sliding glacier

    B. gravity acting upon the loose rocks and dirt in the area surrounding the glacier

    C. water refreezing in the rock crevasses from the melting glacier

Interactive Review

Complete this interactive study guide to review the lesson.

Weathering is the natural process that disintegrates and decomposes rocks. Physical weathering mechanically breaks down rocks. Chemical weathering breaks down rock by chemical reactions or processes such as dissolving rock in water.

A. List and describe different types of physical and chemical weathering.

Erosion is the process by which wind, water, ice, or gravity transport weathered materials from one location to another. Deposition occurs when materials are laid down by wind, water, ice, or gravity.

B. Explain how wind and water can contribute to weathering, but are also agents of erosion and deposition.

Weathering, erosion, and deposition can occur in minutes or over millions of years. Changes can be very large and noticeable, or small and seemingly insignificant.

C. Describe the time and spacial scale related to erosion and deposition.

The Rock Cycle

Arches National Park in Utah is known for its beautiful sandstone arches.

By the end of this lesson . . .

you will be able to describe the processes that form various types of rock and how they involve the cycling of matter and the flow of energy.

Go online to view the digital version of the Hands-On Lab for this lesson and to download additional lab resources.

CAN YOU EXPLAIN IT?

How was the rock in this image of the Grand Canyon formed and shaped over time?

The Colorado River flows through the Grand Canyon. The variety of rocks that make up the Grand Canyon were formed and shaped over long periods of time.

1. Look closely at the rock layers lining the Grand Canyon in the picture. How did these rock layers form? Did these rock layers always look the way they do now?

EVIDENCE NOTEBOOK As you explore the lesson, gather evidence to help explain how the Grand Canyon formed and changed over time.

Comparing Minerals and Rocks

Many parts of Earth are made up of solid rock. There are many types of rock beyond the layered rock that makes up the walls of the Grand Canyon. Other rocks include volcanic boulders, granite cliff faces, and gravel you see every day. Although rocks may differ, the key ingredients of rocks are minerals. To understand how rocks form, you must understand mineral formation as well as which minerals make up different kinds of rocks.

Different colors and textures can be seen in this rock found near the edge of a lake in Sweden.

2. What colors and textures can you see on this rock? Do you think the composition of this rock is the same throughout? Why or why not?

Minerals

A **mineral** is a naturally occurring and usually inorganic solid. It has a definite chemical composition and an orderly internal structure. A mineral's properties depend on the kinds of atoms or molecules that make up the mineral. The conditions under which the mineral forms also affect a mineral's properties. Minerals form by different natural processes. Some minerals form when magma cools. Magma is molten rock inside Earth. As magma cools, the atoms join together to form different minerals. Minerals also form as lava cools. Lava is molten rock on Earth's surface.

Minerals can also form when temperature and pressure within Earth cause the atoms in existing minerals to reorganize, forming a new mineral. When substances that are dissolved in liquid water are left behind as water molecules evaporate, minerals also form.

Minerals are made up of crystals. A crystal is a solid with its atoms or molecules arranged in a repeating pattern. The way the crystal forms determines its size. Some crystals are very large and some can only be seen with a microscope.

This cave in Mexico was once full of water. Over millions of years, dissolved minerals in the water slowly formed these gypsum crystals. These are now considered to be the largest mineral crystals in the world!

3. What is a likely explanation of how these gypsum crystals formed?

  A. intense pressure within Earth

  B. magma cooling over time

  C. evaporation of water

Rocks

Where do rocks come from? Some rocks come from other rocks! Over long periods of time, natural processes change one type of rock into another type of rock. For example, weathering can break down rocks into smaller particles called sediment. Over time, the sediment can be deposited in layers in low-lying areas. This process is called deposition. Eventually, sediment may cement together and form new rock.

Rocks can also form when old rock is buried beneath layers of sediment and other rocks. The weight of the rock or the layers of sediment on top of it puts pressure on the buried rock. Beneath Earth's surface, pressure and temperature increase with depth. If the pressure and temperature are high enough, the minerals in a rock can change into new types of minerals. Then a new type of rock forms. Very deep below Earth's surface, rock gets hot enough to melt and form magma. Magma can eventually cool and solidify to form new rock.

4. What role do you think the different materials and environment play in the appearance of rocks?

This rock is made up of layers of sand that were pressed together and then cemented over time.

This rock is made up of light and dark bands of minerals that were chemically changed from their original form by intense pressure and temperature.

EVIDENCE NOTEBOOK
5. What characteristics do you see in the rocks that form the layers of the Grand Canyon? List these in your notebook.

This rock formed when magma cooled far beneath Earth's surface.

Identify Types of Rock

6. **Discuss** With a partner, write some observations of the rock formation in the picture. What do you notice about the rock and its surroundings? How might this rock have formed?

_____

_____

_____

_____

_____

7. This rock's formation likely resulted from changes in
   temperature / pressure.

Relating Igneous Rocks to the Earth System

Igneous Rock

Cooling magma below ground and cooling lava above ground both form **igneous rocks.** Magma cools below ground in large chambers, in cracks, or between surrounding rock layers. Intrusive igneous rock forms when magma pushes, or intrudes, into the rock below Earth's surface and cools. Extrusive igneous rock forms when lava erupts, or is extruded, onto Earth's surface. Extrusive igneous rock is common at the sides and base of volcanoes.

Lava flows often cool quickly, hardening into rock.

The mineral composition of igneous rocks depends on the chemical make-up of the magma or lava that formed it and on how quickly that magma or lava cooled. Some igneous rocks are made up of many types of minerals. Other igneous rocks have fewer minerals in their make-up.

8. **Discuss** Do you think that the rock in the picture took more or less time to cool than rocks formed from magma beneath Earth's surface? Together with a partner, discuss why you think your conclusion is correct.

Geological Processes

The processes on Earth that form rock take such a long time that it is hard to imagine that they happen continuously. Rock that is on and inside Earth was most likely magma in the past. Likewise, rock that exists now may eventually end up back below Earth's crust. Then it may melt to form magma. These processes in the rock cycle may take hundreds of millions of years.

The flow of energy and matter that forms most rock may not be noticeable. However, if you have ever seen video of an erupting volcano, you have seen a few moments of the process of rock formation.

Lava from a volcanic eruption flows through a tropical forest in Hawaii.

Explore ONLINE!

9. What happens to the matter in rock when it melts beneath Earth's surface? How does the melting process eventually lead to igneous rock forming?

Hands-On Lab
Model Crystal Formation

How do crystals form? You will use salt to observe crystal formation and draw conclusions about the factors that affect crystal size.

Salt is found in natural bodies of water all over the world, especially in oceans and in some inland lakes. When salt water evaporates or changes temperature, salt crystals may form.

MATERIALS
- three beakers, 250 mL
- Epsom salts
- graduated cylinder, 100 mL
- hot plate
- small saucepan
- spoon or stirring rod
- tongs
- 3 test tubes, tempered glass
- hot gloves, terrycloth

Procedure

STEP 1 Add the following to each of the three beakers until each is $\frac{2}{3}$ full:
- beaker 1—water and ice cubes
- beaker 2—water at room temperature
- beaker 3—hot tap water

STEP 2 In a small saucepan, mix 90–100 g of Epsom salts in 120 mL of water. Heat the mixture on a hot plate over low heat. Do not let the mixture boil. Stir the mixture with a spoon or stirring rod until all crystals dissolve.

STEP 3 Using a graduated cylinder, carefully pour equal amounts of the Epsom salts mixture into three test tubes. Use tongs to steady the test tubes as you pour. Drop a few crystals of Epsom salt into each test tube. Then gently shake them. Place a test tube into each beaker.

STEP 4 Cool the test tubes for 15 minutes. Observe what happens. Create a table and record your observations during those 15 minutes. You may write or draw what you observe.

Beaker Observations – 15 minutes		
Beaker 1	Beaker 2	Beaker 3

Analysis

STEP 5 In which beaker did the largest crystals form? How did the temperature and the amount of time affect the size of the crystals?

Time Scale

The time scale for the formation of igneous rocks varies from minutes to hundreds of thousands of years. When igneous rock forms below Earth's surface, the magma is well insulated by surrounding rock, so it cools very slowly. The longer the cooling takes, the more time crystals have to grow. Rocks formed under these conditions generally have large, visible crystals. These rocks are described as "coarse-grained." Examples of igneous rocks that form below Earth's surface are granite and diorite.

On the other hand, magma that reaches Earth's surface, now called lava, cools very quickly when exposed to air. Since there is little time for crystals to form, these rocks are made up of very small crystals. These rocks are said to be "fine-grained." Basalt and andesite are common igneous rocks that are formed on Earth's surface.

Rocks with the same chemistry can have very different appearances when they cool at different rates. Remember: slow cooling results in larger crystals. Fast cooling results in smaller crystals. Super-fast cooling of magma can result in no crystals at all. Obsidian (ahb•SID•ee•uhn) is an igneous rock that cools so rapidly that no crystals form. Obsidian is glassy in appearance and is called volcanic glass.

dolerite   granite   basalt

These igneous rocks cooled at different rates.

10. Compare the pictures of the igneous rocks. Which of the three rocks shows evidence of the longest cooling process? What evidence do you see to support your answer?

Igneous Rock in the Geosphere

Extrusive igneous rock, such as basalt, is easily found on Earth's surface. This is where it formed. Intrusive igneous rock is located beneath Earth's surface, where it formed. However, not all intrusive rock remains underground. For example, large regions of Earth's crust are pushed toward the surface during a process called uplift. Then, the intrusive igneous rock may be exposed at Earth's surface if the layers above are eroded. The Rockies, the largest mountain range of Western North America, is made mostly of intrusive igneous rock, especially granite.

Igneous Rock

The igneous rock columns making up Devil's Tower, Wyoming, show the result of magma forcing its way up toward Earth's surface. Geologists hypothesize that the columns formed underground. The columns later became exposed after the surrounding rock eroded away.

Quick-cooling igneous rock often has a spongy appearance because the lava contained bubbles of gas. This leaves pockets of air in the rock. Pumice is an example of this type of igneous rock and can be light enough to hold above your head with little effort.

11. Compare and contrast the two rock formations shown above. What do these formations have in common as related to energy flow in the Earth system?

Observe How Igneous Rock Forms and Changes

As with all rocks, igneous rocks can be weathered by wind, water, and organisms. Climatic change may also be a factor in the weathering of rocks. For example, as glaciers grow and shrink during ice ages, the granite of massive mountains may be weathered and eroded.

Half Dome

12. Order the events that likely led to the formation of Half Dome. Write numbers 1–4 on the lines to order the events.

___ The granite was uplifted with the surrounding rock.

___ A glacier moved a large part of the granite.

___ A pool of magma cooled underground and formed granite rock.

___ The surrounding rock was weathered and eroded.

One of the iconic rock formations found in Yosemite National Park, California, is Half Dome. It is made of intrusive igneous granite that has weathered with time.

Relating Sedimentary Rocks to the Earth System

Sedimentary Rock

When sediments are compacted or are cemented together by new minerals, **sedimentary rock** is formed. This process is more gradual than the processes that form the igneous rocks. Like the name suggests, sedimentary rock is made of sediment. The mineral "glue" that cements sediment into rock comes from solids that are left behind when solutions that bathe the sediment dry up. For example, the mineral quartz helps to solidify sandstone.

Sedimentary rocks are named according to the size and type of fragments they contain. For example, one type of sedimentary rock called mudstone is made up mostly of cemented mud particles.

Some sedimentary rock, like this breccia (BREHCH-ee-uh) is made up of large, compacted rock fragments.

13. Which layer of rock is oldest in the picture of sandstone at the right? Why do you think so?

Sedimentary rock may form in distinct layers. The layers can be different colors and thicknesses, depending on the type and amount of sediment settling over a given time.

Geological Processes

How does sediment get pressed together, or compacted, and then cemented? Often these processes happen when the weight of higher layers of soil and sediment press down on lower layers of sediment. At the same time, dissolved minerals solidify between sediment pieces and cement them together.

Sedimentary rocks may also form from the remains of fossils of once-living plants and animals. For example, when layer upon layer of plant material is buried, compacted, and exposed to the higher temperatures and pressures beneath Earth's surface, its atoms rearrange. Eventually, peat forms. Then, at a much later time, coal forms.

Sedimentary rock, however, does not always form from layers of sediment. Sometimes it forms as minerals are deposited. Sedimentary minerals form when the water that carries them evaporates. The minerals remain and crystallize. Various kinds of limestone form this way from deposits of calcium carbonate (calcite).

One Way Sedimentary Rock Forms

Sediment and organic materials are deposited over time.	As these materials break down and settle, they form layers.	These layers are compacted and cemented to form sedimentary rock.

14. Select the statements that correctly describe a part of the process shown above.

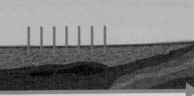 Explore ONLINE!

    A. The oldest rocks are found in the top layers.

    B. Some minerals in the rocks shown were once dissolved in the lake.

    C. Rock layers formed when magma beneath the lake cooled.

    D. The rocks in this scene contain once-living things.

15. Engineer It Sandstone is a type of sedimentary rock that can be formed in a lab environment. How would your knowledge of the formation of sandstone help when designing a machine that could create this rock in a lab?

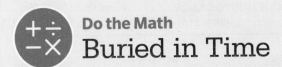

Do the Math

Buried in Time

The height of the travertine shown in the photo is 3 m below the top of the sarcophagus. Assuming a rate of deposition of calcium carbonate of 2 mm/year on average, how many years will it take for the sarcophagus to be completely buried in travertine? Complete the steps below to find out.

In Turkey, calcium-rich hot springs leave behind mineral deposits that cause this rock formation to slowly bury this 2,000-year-old sarcophagus while the rock formation grows.

16. How long will it take for the sarcophagus to be completely buried?

    STEP 1   First, convert meters to millimeters: 3 m = _____ mm

    STEP 2   Then, set up a proportion. Use the variable n to represent the unknown:

$$\frac{2 \text{ mm}}{1 \text{ yr}} = \frac{\boxed{} \text{ mm}}{\boxed{} \text{ yr}}$$

    STEP 3   Solve the proportion.

Time Scale

As you learned in the example of the travertine that is slowly burying the sarcophagus, sedimentary rock forms slowly over time. A person could observe the travertine deposit growing very slowly over a period of years—about 2 cm in 10 years. But the deposition of calcium carbonate out of solution to form travertine is actually one of the faster ways that sedimentary rock can form. Sedimentary rock formed from the compaction and cementation of sediments may take many thousands or even millions of years to form.

Shale may take millions of years to form by compaction and eventual cementation of clay sediments.

17. **Discuss** Look at the images and read about the formation of shale and limestone. Together with a partner, compare and contrast the process of shale and limestone formation.

Limestone is formed by the deposition of calcium carbonate. Limestone stalactites hanging from the ceilings of caves form rapidly when compared to other sedimentary rocks.

Sedimentary Rock in the Geosphere

Sedimentary rock is often identified by its visible layers. Even though you can see these sedimentary rocks, that does not mean they were formed on or near the surface. The pressure needed for compaction of some sedimentary rocks happens under many layers of sediment and rock, over thousands or millions of years.

Water plays a key role in forming, as well as exposing, sedimentary rock. Water contains many dissolved minerals and salts. Water can flow through sediments and leave the minerals and salts behind, which can cement the sediments together. After a sedimentary rock is formed under the surface, uplift can push the rock up toward the surface. Then, weathering and erosion might expose and shape the rock into the formations we see today. For example, over millions of years the Colorado River has helped to shape the Grand Canyon and expose the many colorful layers that make up the canyon walls.

Examples of Sedimentary Rock

Conglomerate rocks are made of large pieces of sediment later cemented together.

The Rainbow Mountains of Gansu Province, China, are sandstone. The different colors and textures are due to differences in the mineral composition and grain size.

The White Cliffs of Dover, England, are made of chalky limestone. They are composed largely of the calcium carbonate shells of tiny ocean-dwelling organisms.

18. Which of these three words applies to all types of sedimentary rock: *weathering, compaction,* or *deposition*? Explain your answer.

EVIDENCE NOTEBOOK

19. Do you see any evidence of sedimentary rock in the Grand Canyon? If so, how long do you think it took to form and how has the rock changed over time?

Identify How Sedimentary Rock Forms and Changes

Like other types of rock, sedimentary rock can be affected by its surroundings. Wind and water can weather and erode sedimentary rock, sometimes exposing new layers.

20. Use what you know to write a series of three events that could have led to the formation of Monument Valley as it appears today.

_____

_____

_____

_____

_____

_____

The sedimentary rock of Monument Valley, Arizona, was formed approximately 300 to 100 million years ago at what was then near sea level. Since then, dramatic uplift has moved the rock to its current position of 2000 m above sea level. Amazingly its horizontal layers are undisturbed! However, rivers that flooded over it at various times over millions of years have carried much of the rock away.

Relating Metamorphic Rocks to the Earth System

Metamorphic Rock

When large changes of temperature, pressure, or both cause the texture and mineral content of existing rock to change over millions of years, **metamorphic rock** forms. Contact with hot fluids can also cause changes to rock. *Metamorphosis* is another word for this change. Rocks undergo metamorphism when their temperatures typically reach ranges of 200 °C to 1200 °C.

Imagine a rock that is buried deep in Earth's crust. The temperature and pressure are very high. Over millions of years, the solid rock changes to a different kind of rock.

Gneiss (NYS) is a metamorphic rock. It forms at high temperatures deep within Earth's crust.

21. **Discuss** Together with a partner, discuss why the gneiss rock shown above has both light bands and dark bands.

Geological Processes

Any rock—whether igneous, sedimentary, or metamorphic—can be exposed to physical or chemical conditions that cause the rock's minerals to change and form new minerals and then become a new metamorphic rock. Each type of metamorphic rock forms under a certain range of temperature and pressure, and it contains particular kinds of minerals.

Metamorphic Rock May Form Near a Magma Chamber

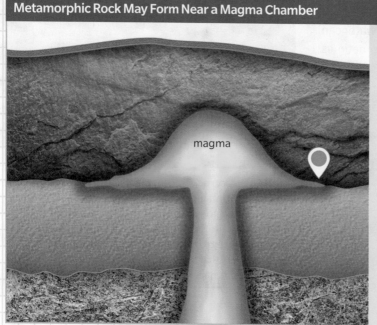

magma

Hornfels is a metamorphic rock that forms in the zone of shale closest to magma, where the shale is exposed to very high temperatures.

Metamorphic Rock Formation

All three kinds of rock—sedimentary, igneous, or metamorphic—can be changed into new metamorphic rock. Increased temperature and pressure can cause changes to both the physical and chemical make-up of the rock. These changes result in the formation of a new type of rock—a metamorphic rock different from the original rock. The kind of metamorphic rock that forms depends on the parent rock.

Metamorphic rock can form in areas that are in contact with or close to a magma chamber. The intense heat of the magma chamber can change the minerals in nearby rock. Rock can also undergo metamorphosis when it is buried deep enough in Earth that a large region of rock is subjected to intense heat and pressure. In this situation, large areas of rock can be changed into different types of rock.

An example of metamorphic rock transformation is quartzite. Quartzite forms when sandstone, a sedimentary rock, is exposed to high temperature and pressure. This causes the sand grains to grow larger and the spaces between the sand grains to disappear.

Before	Metamorphosis	After
shale 	Slate results from exposing shale to moderate pressure and temperature increases over a very long period of time—perhaps millions of years. Slate is a metamorphic rock in which the minerals have become squeezed into flat, sheet-like layers.	slate 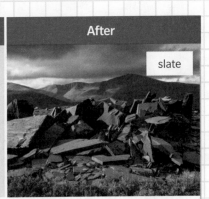
slate	Metamorphic rocks can change into other types of metamorphic rock. Slate can become phyllite when it is exposed to increased temperature and pressure. Tiny plates of a sparkling mineral called mica formed during metamorphosis. This gives phyllite a slight sheen.	phyllite 
basalt	Basalt is an igneous rock that can change into amphibolite when exposed to temperatures between 500 °C and 850 °C. Amphibolite has grains coarse enough for individual minerals to be seen.	amphibolite 

22. Circle the answer that best completes each statement.

   A. A sedimentary rock is most likely to change into metamorphic rock after heating / erosion / deposition.

   B. Metamorphic rocks are usually / sometimes / never produced by changes to other metamorphic rock.

Time Scale

The formation of metamorphic rock is generally a very slow process because the change process involves rock in its solid state. The process to form coarser-grained metamorphic rocks with larger mineral crystals, such as gneiss, may take tens of millions of years.

23. How does the time it takes to form metamorphic rock compare to the time it takes to form extrusive igneous rock?

24. What happens to the minerals in rocks that undergo metamorphism?

Metamorphic Rocks in the Geosphere

Since metamorphic rock forms deep in the earth, how are you able to see it? The ridges making up much of the Appalachian Mountains are metamorphic rock. This rock formed when the North American plate and the African plate crashed together millions of years ago. Metamorphic rock may be moved to the surface by uplift or after erosion carves away some top layers of igneous or sedimentary rock.

Some rocks are easy to identify as metamorphic. When a metamorphic rock forms, pressure on the rock may force the mineral crystals into parallel layers. These layers can show up as dark and light bands. Other kinds of metamorphic rocks will not show this kind of structure. Instead, these rocks will have large grains that are arranged in an unstructured manner.

greenschist

Schist is often categorized by color. Greenschists, like this one, form under high pressure and high temperature, as found far below Earth's crust. Blueschists form under high pressure but relatively low temperature.

gneiss

Exposing schist to higher temperature and pressure can eventually cause its minerals to separate into alternating bands of light and dark as it transforms into another metamorphic rock called gneiss.

25. **Discuss** Is it possible for metamorphic rock to form on Earth's surface? Together with a partner, discuss your answer and explain your reasoning.

marble

This marble formed beneath the ocean floor millions of years ago. It was uplifted and carved by erosion into vast cliffs. When this marble was formed, the calcite crystals in the original limestone grew, filling the air spaces in the limestone. This resulted in harder and longer lasting marble. Marble is not as hard as granite. However, marble is chosen as a building material for grand monuments due to its beauty.

Describe How Metamorphic Rock Forms

Metamorphic rock often shows evidence of the strong forces that helped form it. These forces can even change metamorphic rock into different kinds of metamorphic rock. Uneven pressures applied to rock may cause a rock to be squeezed or stretched only in certain areas. This uneven stretching may result in the bands of minerals being folded into a wavy pattern.

Metamorphic rocks, just like igneous and sedimentary rock, can also be weathered over time. The weathering may expose mineral patterns.

This metamorphic rock was exposed after glacial movement eroded part of it away. The wavy bands of minerals are a clue to the intense forces experienced during its metamorphism.

26. Use what you know about the formation of metamorphic rock to describe three events that could have led to the formation of this folded rock as it appears today.

_____

_____

_____

_____

_____

_____

Modeling the Rock Cycle

Although rocks seem solid and unchanging, they can be changed by temperatures and pressure beneath Earth's surface and weathering on Earth's surface. As a result, rocks undergo changes. These changes sometimes form new kinds of rock. This series of processes, in which rocks change from one type to another, is called the rock cycle. The rock cycle process is one way that matter is recycled on Earth.

The action of waves has broken up shells at the beach into tiny fragments.

This limestone was extracted from the ocean floor.

This marble was cut from a quarry several miles inland.

27. These photos could be connected by processes in the rock cycle. Describe what processes could turn the shell fragments into limestone and then marble. Then describe a process in the rock cycle that the marble in the quarry might undergo in the future.

The Rock Cycle

Think about all the processes that form the three kinds of rock—igneous, sedimentary, and metamorphic—and the factors that influence those processes. How are these processes related to each other? How do they recycle matter on Earth?

The processes that form different kinds of rock and recycle matter on Earth do not have one defined pathway. The pathways are more like a web. You can use a model of the rock cycle to show how the processes that form different kinds of rocks are related.

28. Circle the energy source for these processes in the rock cycle.

A. Melting and cooling: sun / Earth's interior

B. Erosion, deposition, and cementation: sun / Earth's interior

C. Changing temperature and pressure: sun / Earth's interior

29. Complete the rock cycle diagram by writing sedimentary rock or igneous rock. Metamorphic rock has been filled in for you.

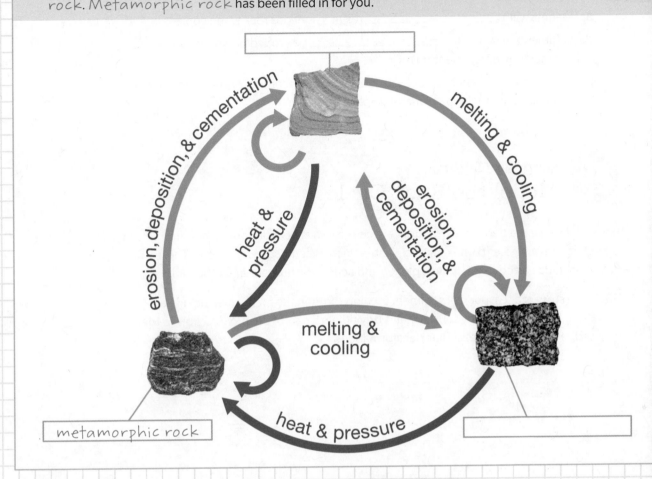

30. Discuss Together with a partner, describe how this rock cycle model provides a visual representation of the cycling of matter through Earth's systems.

Paths in the Rock Cycle

With pressure and temperature changes, sedimentary rock may become metamorphic rock. Sedimentary rock may melt and cool to form igneous rock. Or sedimentary rock at Earth's surface may break down into sediment that will form new sedimentary rock.

Igneous rock can change directly into metamorphic rock while still beneath Earth's surface, or it might melt and then cool again to form a new igneous rock. Igneous rock at Earth's surface can be weathered to form sediments that form sedimentary rock.

Metamorphic rock can melt and form magma. The magma cools to form igneous rock. Metamorphic rock can also be changed by temperature and pressure to form a different type of metamorphic rock. Weathering can change metamorphic rock into sediments that will become sedimentary rock.

EVIDENCE NOTEBOOK

31. How did the processes in the rock cycle play a role in the formation of the Grand Canyon? Record your evidence.

32. Write *always*, *sometimes*, or *never* to complete the statements.

  A. Igneous rock will _____ change as a result of temperature and pressure.

  B. Magma will _____ result in igneous rock when cooled.

  C. Sedimentary rock will _____ be eroded before becoming another type of sedimentary rock.

  D. Metamorphic rock will _____ become an igneous rock before it becomes another type of metamorphic rock.

Language SmArts
Model the Rock Cycle

Rocks define a large part of Earth's surface. Those rocks are continuously changing as a result of the processes of the rock cycle. Other factors can also change rock. These factors include earthquakes, floods, plants, and actions by humans and other animals.

33. Tell a story of a teaspoon of sediment moving through the rock cycle. Include a discussion of the energy source that is driving each part of the process. Follow the sediment through at least four transformations.

_____

_____

_____

_____

_____

_____

_____

34. Draw In the space provided, draw a rock cycle diagram to go with your story.

Continue Your Exploration

Name: _____   Date: _____

Check out the path below or go online to choose one of the other paths shown.

Coal Mining

- **Hands-On Labs** ✋
- **Geodes**
- **Propose Your Own Path**

Go online to choose one of these other paths.

Minerals and rocks are used for many purposes, such as building homes, paving roads, and manufacturing consumer items. Before they can be used, rocks and minerals must be mined, or removed from the ground. Some materials are mined from large open pits, called quarries. Others must be removed from deep, underground tunnels.

Some common mineral resources are granite, limestone, marble, sand, gravel, gypsum, iron, and copper. Some rocks, such as coal, are burned for heat and to generate energy. Coal is burned in power plants to release energy that is converted to electricity. In fact, more than 90% of the coal mined in the United States is used to generate electricity.

The original source of the energy stored in coal is the sun. Hundreds of millions of years ago, remains of plants that died were buried beneath sand, rock, or mud. This created a pocket of carbon-rich materials that were trapped in layers of sediment and rock. Over time, temperature and pressure from these sediments changed the buried plant materials into the coal that we mine today.

coal seam

Coal seams are layers of sedimentary rock that are formed from organic matter over millions of years.

Continue Your Exploration

1. Based on how it is formed, what type of rock is coal?

   A. sedimentary

   B. igneous

   C. metamorphic

2. Explain why you think mining for coal almost always requires miners to dig deep into the ground.

3. Draw a model of how the flow of energy relates to the formation, mining, and burning of coal by humans as an energy source.

4. **Collaborate** Discuss with a classmate how mining for coal may have changed over the years. Research different ways coal is mined. What processes are best used to extract the coal? Provide evidence for your argument.

Can You Explain It?

Name: _____   Date: _____

Look back at the Grand Canyon rock layers.

How was the rock in this image of the Grand Canyon formed and shaped over time?

EVIDENCE NOTEBOOK

Refer to the notes in your Evidence Notebook to help you construct an explanation for how the rock layers formed and were shaped over time.

1. State your claim. Make sure your claim fully explains how the rocks in the Grand Canyon formed and were shaped over time.

2. Summarize the evidence you have gathered to support your claim and explain your reasoning.

Checkpoints

Answer the following questions to check your understanding of the lesson.

Use the photo to answer Questions 3–5.

3. What do you observe in this rock? Choose all that apply.

    A. Crystals of different sizes

    B. Crystals of different colors

    C. Cemented sediments

4. Based on your observations, in which general category would you place this rock?

    A. Sedimentary

    B. Metamorphic

    C. Intrusive igneous

    D. Extrusive igneous

5. In which order did these events most likely occur during this rock's formation?
   Write numbers 1–4 on the lines to order the events.

    ___ Magma began cooling.

    ___ Uplift moved the rock to the surface.

    ___ Heat from Earth's interior formed magma.

    ___ Crystals formed in the rock.

Use the photo to answer Questions 6–7.

6. Based on your observations, in which general category would you place this rock?

    A. Sedimentary

    B. Metamorphic

    C. Intrusive igneous

    D. Extrusive igneous

7. What type of rock fragments could be part of this rock? Choose all that apply.

    A. Sedimentary

    B. Metamorphic

    C. Intrusive igneous

    D. Extrusive igneous

Interactive Review

Complete this section to review the main concepts of the lesson.

Rocks are composed of minerals.

A. What characteristics do minerals have in common?

The three rock types are igneous, sedimentary, and metamorphic rock.

B. What do all rocks have in common? How is the formation of the three rock types similar? How is the formation different?

Igneous, sedimentary, and metamorphic rocks are all part of the rock cycle.

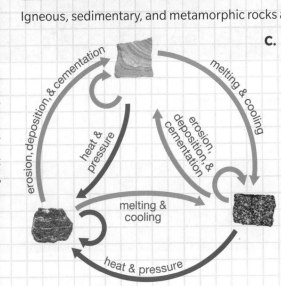

C. Use the rock cycle diagram to explain how a sedimentary rock could become a metamorphic rock.

Earth's Plates

This underwater canyon in Iceland is a result of two pieces of Earth's surface pulling apart.

By the end of this lesson . . .

you will be able to analyze data to provide evidence for plate tectonics.

Go *online* to view the digital version of the Hands-On Lab for this lesson and to download additional lab resources.

CAN YOU EXPLAIN IT?

How might this island have appeared overnight?

In November 2013 off the coast of Japan, an island formed virtually overnight. The view quickly changed from calm Pacific waters to violent volcanic eruptions. By the next morning, an entirely new island had appeared. The new island continued to grow for about two years.

▷ Explore
ONLINE!

1. What explanation can you suggest for how an island could suddenly appear? Could this happen anywhere, or might there be something special about the location that made this possible?

2. **Draw** Include a drawing to illustrate your explanation.

EVIDENCE NOTEBOOK As you explore the lesson, gather evidence to help explain how an island could suddenly appear.

Analyzing Continental Data

Continental Observations

Long ago, people noticed that some continents, such as Africa and South America, looked as if they could fit together. Explorers also discovered rocks and landforms of the same ages and compositions on different continents. They also found fossils of the same plants and animals across continents. What could explain these findings?

Fossil Data

This map shows where four types of fossils have been discovered on different continents.

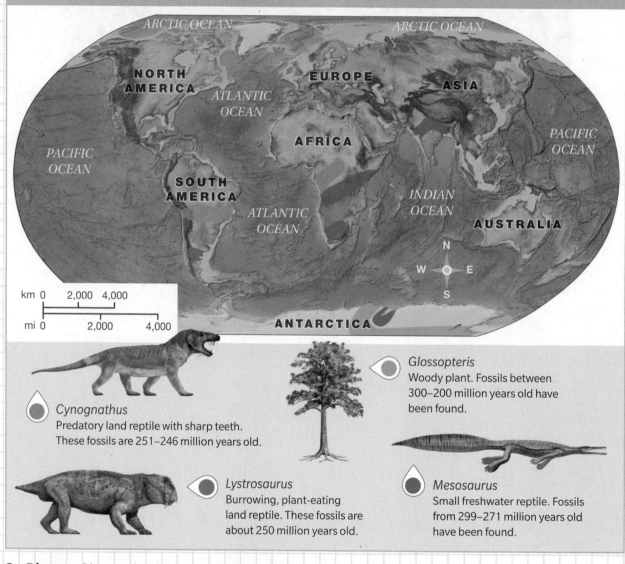

Glossopteris
Woody plant. Fossils between 300–200 million years old have been found.

Cynognathus
Predatory land reptile with sharp teeth. These fossils are 251–246 million years old.

Lystrosaurus
Burrowing, plant-eating land reptile. These fossils are about 250 million years old.

Mesosaurus
Small freshwater reptile. Fossils from 299–271 million years old have been found.

3. **Discuss** Observe the shapes and locations of the continents. Do you think they have always been in the same locations, or do they move? Explain your thinking.

4. Fill in the table with your observations as you explore the map. Think about the following points:

- What was the plant or animal like?
- When and where did it live according to the map?
- Use the scale bar to estimate how far apart fossils of the same type were found.

Fossil Data Observations	
Fossil Type	Observations and Notes
Cynognathus	
Glossopteris	
Lystrosaurus	• Land reptile • Lived around 250 million years ago. • Lived in Africa, Asia, and Antarctica. • Fossils in Africa are about 3,000 km from those in Asia and about 7,000 km from those in Antarctica.
Mesosaurus	

Fossil Data

Fossils are the traces or remains of organisms that lived long ago. Fossils are most commonly preserved in rock. Fossils may be skeletons, burrows, footprints, or body parts such as shells that have been replaced by minerals.

Fossils can give us clues about what the environment was like when the organism was alive. For example, fish fossils indicate that an aquatic environment existed. Palm leaf fossils mean a tropical environment existed. Scientists have found fossils of trees and dinosaurs in Antarctica, so the climate there must have been warmer in the past.

Mesosaurus fossils like this one have been found in both South America and Africa.

Landform Data

Did you notice how the dashed lines on the map look like the edges of two puzzle pieces? These dashed lines follow along the continental shelves of North America, South America, Europe, and Africa. Look at the diagram. A *continental shelf* is the edge of a continent that is underwater. Just past the edge of the shelf is a steep drop-off into the deep ocean.

Look at the mountain ranges shown on the map. The rocks that make up these mountains have been analyzed by geologists. It was found that many of the rocks are the same age and made up of the same materials. These pieces of evidence led to the conclusion that parts of these mountain ranges formed at the same time.

Continental Shelf

A continental shelf is the edge of a continent that is covered with water.

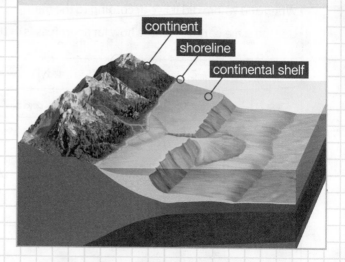

Matching Landforms Across the Atlantic Ocean

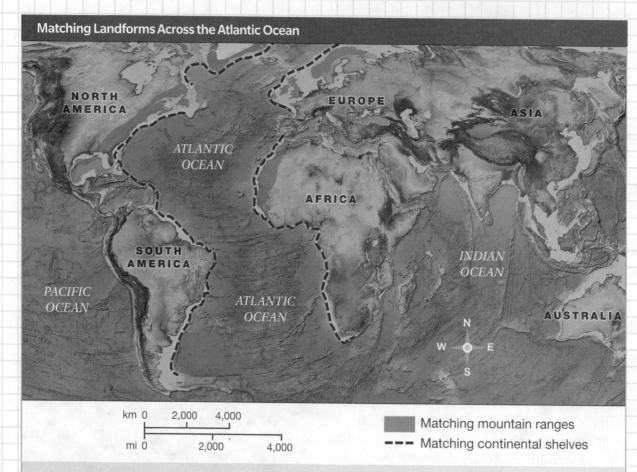

km 0   2,000   4,000

mi 0   2,000   4,000

Matching mountain ranges

– – – Matching continental shelves

Matching Mountain Ranges
Look at the mountain ranges within the colored area on the map. Many parts of these mountains match in age and composition. Scientists have concluded that the mountains formed around the same time.

Matching Continental Shelves
The dashed outlines trace along continental shelves that were measured and mapped in the 1960s. It was found that the continental shelves match up even more closely than the shorelines of the continents.

5. Fill in the table with your observations as you explore the map.

Landform Data Observations	
Data	Observations and Notes
Mountain Ranges	
Continental Shelves	

Explain Your Observations

Since the late 1800s, people have attempted to explain the matching fossils and landforms on the continents. One idea was that land bridges once connected the continents, allowing plants and animals to spread. Some thought that the entire planet expanded and tore the continents apart, then water filled the spaces between them. Others thought the continents were once part of a single landmass surrounded by a large ocean, and then the landmass broke up and the pieces drifted apart.

6. Recall your discussion about whether the continents have moved over time. Compare it to the ideas listed here. Have you changed your mind? Do your observations of fossils and landforms support any of these ideas? Explain.

_____

_____

_____

_____

_____

_____

_____

_____

_____

_____

_____

_____

_____

Analyzing Oceanic Data

Discoveries in the Ocean

In the mid-1900s, new technology allowed scientists to map the ocean floor. They found a giant continuous mountain range they called the *mid-ocean ridge*. One part, the Mid-Atlantic Ridge, runs along the entire middle of the Atlantic Ocean. Scientists also found *deep-ocean trenches*, which are the deepest valleys on Earth's surface.

Mid-Ocean Ridges and Deep-Ocean Trenches

This map shows the locations of mid-ocean ridges in red and deep-ocean trenches in yellow. The diagram beneath the map shows what these features look like.

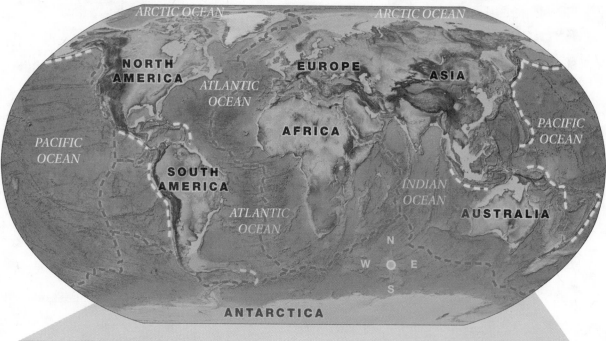

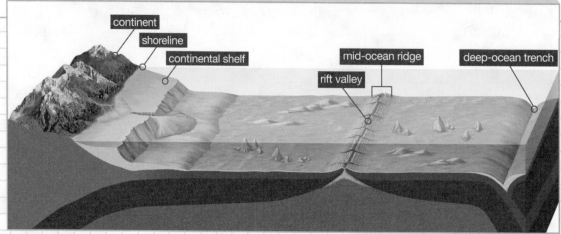

7. **Discuss** With a partner, look at the map of mid-ocean ridges and deep-ocean trenches. Compare this to the maps of fossils and landforms. Note any patterns you see.

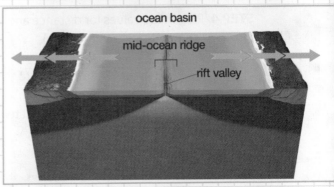

The Mid-Atlantic Ridge can be seen above water in Iceland!

Sea-Floor Spreading and Mid-Ocean Ridges

Did you know that the oceans change over millions of years? Oceans form by the process of *sea-floor spreading*. First, forces deep within Earth stretch the crust apart and eventually form a *rift valley*. This stretching results in earthquakes and volcanic eruptions. Eruptions add new rock. As long as forces continue to stretch the crust, the rift valley widens. The valley can fill with water to become a narrow sea, sometimes called a *linear sea*. The linear sea eventually widens enough to become an ocean basin.

How did the mid-ocean ridge you see in the diagram form? The ocean floor moves away from a rift valley on either side, like two conveyor belts. As it moves away, it becomes cooler and denser and sinks deeper beneath the water. Closer to the rift valley, the ocean floor is an elevated ridge because the newly formed rock there is warmer and less dense. This elevated ridge is the mid-ocean ridge.

8. Complete the captions to describe how an ocean basin forms by the process of sea-floor spreading.

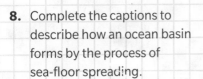

WORD BANK
- rift valley
- linear sea
- ocean basin

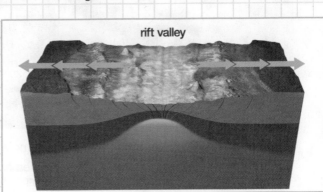

rift valley

A. Earth's crust is stretched by forces within Earth. Here, a ___rift valley___ forms and volcanic eruptions occur.

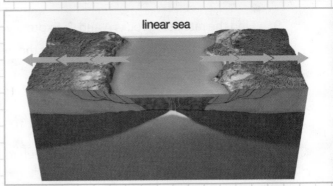

linear sea

B. As forces continue stretching the land on either side of the rift valley, the area widens. It fills with water to form a (an) _____.

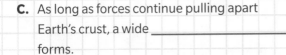

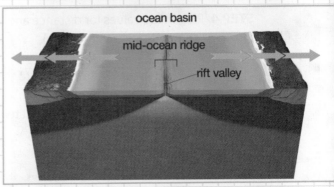

ocean basin

mid-ocean ridge

rift valley

C. As long as forces continue pulling apart Earth's crust, a wide _____ forms.

Do the Math
Calculate the Rate of Sea-Floor Spreading

How fast does the Atlantic Ocean grow? To find out, we can calculate the rate of sea-floor spreading. The map shows the age of the ocean floor and three rock samples. For example, rock B is 55 million years old. So is any rock on the red line labeled "55." Rock B formed 55 million years ago at the ridge, then traveled to its current location. Rock C is now at the ridge. To find the rate of spreading, first estimate the distance between rocks B and C by using the scale bar. Divide that by the difference in their ages. In other words, rate is

distance divided by time (age difference): $r = \dfrac{d}{t}$. So, $r = \dfrac{200{,}000{,}000 \text{ cm}}{55{,}000{,}000 \text{ y}}$, or about 3.6 $\dfrac{\text{cm}}{\text{y}}$.

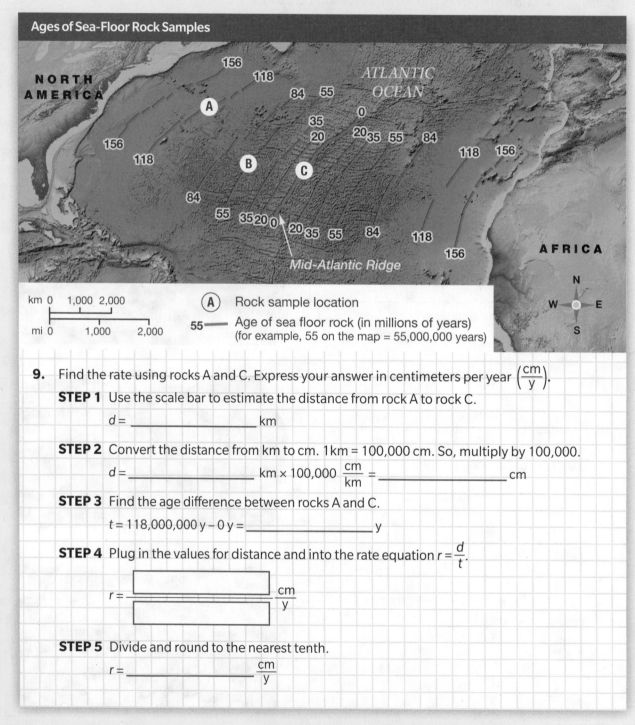

Ages of Sea-Floor Rock Samples

km 0   1,000 2,000
mi 0   1,000   2,000

(A) Rock sample location

55—— Age of sea floor rock (in millions of years)
(for example, 55 on the map = 55,000,000 years)

9. Find the rate using rocks A and C. Express your answer in centimeters per year $\left(\dfrac{\text{cm}}{\text{y}}\right)$.

STEP 1 Use the scale bar to estimate the distance from rock A to rock C.

$d =$ _____ km

STEP 2 Convert the distance from km to cm. 1 km = 100,000 cm. So, multiply by 100,000.

$d =$ _____ km × 100,000 $\dfrac{\text{cm}}{\text{km}}$ = _____ cm

STEP 3 Find the age difference between rocks A and C.

$t = 118{,}000{,}000 \text{ y} - 0 \text{ y} =$ _____ y

STEP 4 Plug in the values for distance and into the rate equation $r = \dfrac{d}{t}$.

$r = \dfrac{\boxed{}}{\boxed{}} \dfrac{\text{cm}}{\text{y}}$

STEP 5 Divide and round to the nearest tenth.

$r =$ _____ $\dfrac{\text{cm}}{\text{y}}$

Deep-Ocean Trenches

Deep-ocean trenches form where the oceanic part of Earth's outer layer is cool and dense enough to sink into Earth's interior. So, the ocean floor is part of a cycle of matter. New ocean floor forms at mid-ocean ridge. It slowly moves away from the ridge while it cools and becomes denser. Millions of years later, it is recycled as it sinks into Earth at a deep-ocean trench. One day, that recycled rock may rise again at a mid-ocean ridge.

Volcanic mountain chains often run parallel to deep-ocean trenches. This is because sinking slabs of ocean floor cause eruptions parallel to the trench that can build up mountains over time. The motion at trenches also causes earthquakes.

EVIDENCE NOTEBOOK

10. Think about the island that appeared overnight. What processes and features might relate to the formation of an island like this?

Explain the Age of the Ocean Floor

In the mid-1900s, new technology allowed scientists to determine the age of sea-floor rock. They discovered the interesting patterns you see on this map. They also discovered that ocean floor rock is generally much younger than continental rock.

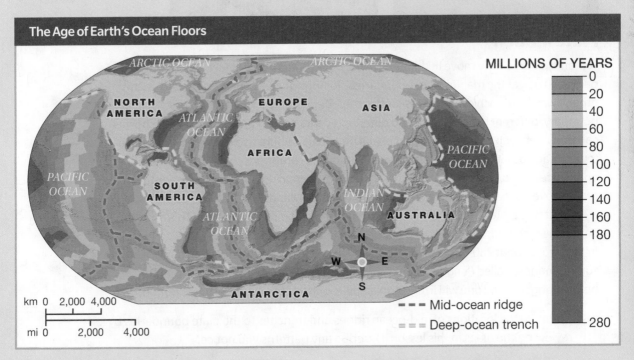

The Age of Earth's Ocean Floors

11. Rock near mid-ocean ridges is the oldest / youngest rock.

12. Compare the age of sea-floor rock near mid-ocean ridges and near trenches. Try to explain these patterns in ocean floor age.

_____

_____

_____

_____

_____

Modeling Earth's Surface

Earth's Broken Surface

Evidence has led scientists to conclude that Earth's entire surface, including the ocean floor and the continents, is broken into large moving pieces. These pieces are called **tectonic plates**. The plates fit together like a jigsaw puzzle to form Earth's outer shell, but the pieces are thousands of kilometers wide and hundreds of kilometers thick!

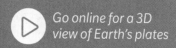 *Go online for a 3D view of Earth's plates*

Earth's thin and rigid outer shell is broken into giant moving pieces called tectonic plates.

Plate Motion

Tectonic plates slowly move in different ways. Most plates move at just a few centimeters per year. Look at the map of plate boundaries. Tectonic plates can move toward each other, away from each other, or past each other. Depending on the type of motion at a boundary, different features form and different events occur. For example, ocean basins can grow between continents as two plates pull apart. Where two oceanic plates move toward each other, the denser plate sinks. This causes eruptions that build up material on the ocean floor, over time forming a volcanic mountain. Eventually, the mountain may grow above the ocean's surface to become a volcanic island.

Tectonic plates have been moving for hundreds of millions of years. This motion has formed, shifted, and destroyed features on Earth's surface, including the continents. In fact, from about 280–245 million years ago, all the continents were joined into a supercontinent called *Pangaea* (pan•JEE•uh). There were several supercontinents before Pangaea, and one will likely form again hundreds of millions of years from now.

13. Compare the locations of mid-ocean ridges and trenches to the plate boundaries by reviewing the maps in this lesson. Describe any patterns you notice.

 EVIDENCE NOTEBOOK

14. What type of plate motion is associated with the formation of most volcanic islands? Explain.

Plate Boundaries and Surface Features

Each colored line represents a different type of plate boundary. The diagrams show the different features that result from the different types of plate motion at each boundary.

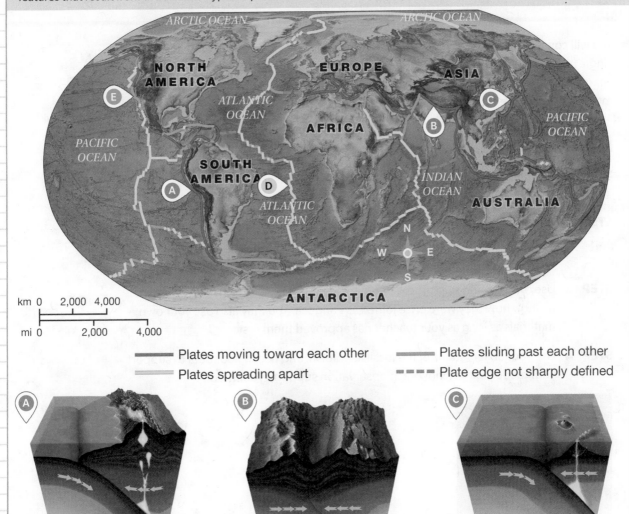

km 0   2,000   4,000

mi 0   2,000   4,000

——— Plates moving toward each other   ——— Plates sliding past each other

——— Plates spreading apart   ----- Plate edge not sharply defined

Ⓐ   Ⓑ   Ⓒ

15. These diagrams show plates moving *toward / away from / past* each other. Where an oceanic plate sinks, deep-ocean trenches, volcanic mountains, or volcanic islands can form. Where two continental plates collide, mountains build up.

Ⓓ

16. Here, two plates move *toward / away from / past* each other. Magma rises in the rift valley that runs along the center of the mid-ocean ridge and causes eruptions.

Ⓔ

17. Here, two plates move *toward / away from / past* each other. This offsets features on the surface. Eruptions do not usually occur here. Earthquakes happen at all plate boundaries.

Model the Movement of Continents

You will construct a model to show how the continents once fit together as a single landmass called Pangaea. Pangaea existed from about 280–245 million years ago. Brainstorm ways you can use the model to show how the continents moved to their current positions.

MATERIALS

- map of continents
- scissors
- animation (provided by your teacher)

Procedure and Analysis

STEP 1 Review the observations you made about the fossils, landforms, and the ocean floor's features and processes.

STEP 2 Think about how your observations can be used to construct your model. For example, think about when the plants and animals from the fossil map lived and where these fossils are now located.

STEP 3 Use the map and scissors to cut out the continents and construct your model to show how they were once joined as Pangaea. You may also use your own materials as long as your teacher has approved them first.

STEP 4 Use your observations of the fossil, landform, and ocean floor data to support your model. Explain how each observation supports your model.

STEP 5 Look at a map of the plate boundaries with the continents in their current positions. Using your model of Pangaea, explore how the plates may have moved to result in the current positions of the continents.

STEP 6 Observe how scientists reconstructed the breakup of Pangaea. Compare this to your model. Record similarities and differences.

245 million years ago

About 245 million years ago, the continents we know today were joined into a single landmass.

135 million years ago

As tectonic plates moved at just a few centimeters a year, this landmass slowly broke apart.

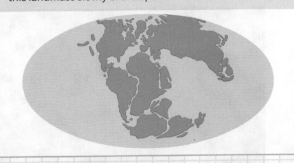

STEP 7 Evaluate your model. Which aspects of plate motion are represented and which are not?

Present Day

Fossils, rocks, and other evidence help us understand how the continents came to be in their current positions.

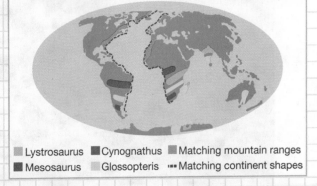

- ■ Lystrosaurus ■ Cynognathus ■ Matching mountain ranges
- ■ Mesosaurus ■ Glossopteris ▪▪▪ Matching continent shapes

Predict Plate Motion

18. Look back to the map of plate boundaries. If the plates continue to move in the same ways they are currently, what will happen to South America and Africa? What is happening to the Atlantic Ocean?

_____

_____

_____

_____

Explaining Plate Motion

You cannot feel it, but the ground beneath you is in constant motion. In fact, you are on top of a moving tectonic plate as you read this! Even though plates move slowly, they can cause sudden events, such as volcanic eruptions and earthquakes.

19. Explore the photos below. Which type of plate motion is responsible for all three of these features?

    A. Plates pushing upward

    B. Plates moving apart

    C. Plates sliding past each other

    D. Plates moving toward each other

This is just one of the 80 islands of Vanuatu (van•wah•TOO). This long chain of volcanic islands runs parallel to a deep-ocean trench.

The West Mata volcano is nearly 1,200 meters deep and lies on the floor of the Pacific Ocean near a deep-ocean trench.

The Himalayas are mountains that have been growing for millions of years. They form a boundary between two countries.

The Theory of Plate Tectonics

Plate tectonics is the theory that describes how Earth's outer shell is broken up into moving tectonic plates. It also explains how plates shape Earth's surface. Some of the first pieces of evidence supporting this theory were matching fossils and landforms on separate continents. Next came discoveries in the ocean, such as sea-floor spreading. Today, additional evidence comes from Global Positioning System (GPS) instruments that directly measure the speeds and directions of Earth's moving plates.

20. Engineer It Models help us understand concepts such as plate tectonics. Think about items you could use to represent tectonic plates or their motion. List or draw two items, explaining how each item represents Earth's plates.

North American plate

Pacific plate

Alaska has a long chain of islands that extends across the ocean. These islands often experience volcanic eruptions and earthquakes.

21. Complete the description. You may want to refer to the other maps in this lesson showing plate boundaries.

The red line below these Alaskan islands shows a plate boundary where the Pacific Plate is sinking beneath the North American Plate. This motion forms a *deep-ocean trench / mid-ocean ridge*. The sinking edge of the Pacific Plate triggers melting that results in eruptions on the North American Plate. Repeated eruptions have built up these *basins / islands.*

EVIDENCE NOTEBOOK

22. As you continue exploring this section, identify the energy source that drives plate motion. How does the flow of energy and cycling of matter relate to the formation of the island from the beginning of the lesson?

Causes of Plate Motion

Energy from deep within Earth drives temperature and density differences in Earth's interior. Along with gravity, this causes the mostly solid interior to slowly cycle. These cycles are called **convection currents**. Earth's outer shell of moving plates is part of this cycle. Where the edge of a plate sinks into Earth, it pulls the rest of the plate along with it. At mid-ocean ridges, plate edges sit higher than the surrounding plates. This puts pressure on the plates and "pushes" them away from the ridge.

How Plates Move

23. Choose from the phrases to label this diagram. You may use a phrase more than once.

| Plates move toward each other | Plates move away from each other |

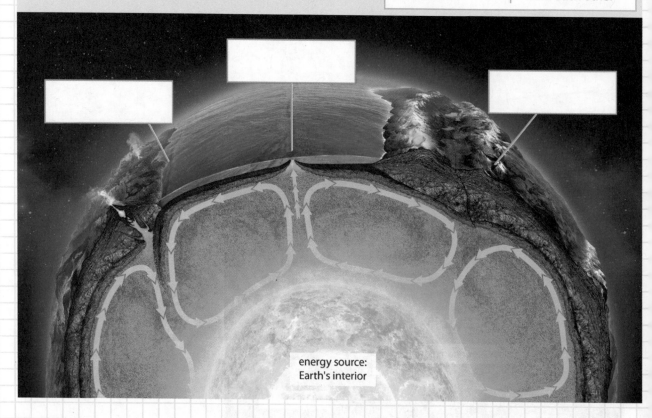

energy source:
Earth's interior

Language SmArts
Cite Evidence for Plate Tectonics

24. Explain how GPS instruments and studies of Earth's fossils, landforms, and ocean floor provide evidence for plate tectonics.

_____

_____

_____

_____

_____

_____

Continue Your Exploration

Name: _____ Date: _____

Check out the path below or go online to choose one of the other paths shown.

People in Science

- **Hands-On Labs** ✋
- **Deep-Sea Resources Debate**
- **Propose Your Own Path**

Go online to choose one of these other paths.

Doug Gibbons, Research Scientist Assistant

In and around Seattle, Washington, earthquakes are a major risk. This is where Doug Gibbons lives and works, not too far from a tectonic plate boundary where one plate is sinking beneath another. The motion at this plate boundary can cause major earthquakes that damage buildings, roads, and cause injury or death.

Part of Doug's job is installing and maintaining instruments that detect earthquakes for the Pacific Northwest Seismic Network (PNSN). He also speaks with the media and schools to inform people about earthquakes and the importance of monitoring them. Doug's favorite part of the job is traveling. He has spent time at the beach, in remote parts of the forest, and even at the tops of volcanoes. However, he occasionally travels to less exciting places, such as dusty basements, to install and check his earthquake instruments.

An Earthquake Warning System

Doug and others at PNSN are working toward building an earthquake warning system that will alert people before shaking occurs. This is one reason the earthquake detection instruments Doug works on are so important. But earthquakes are unpredictable, so how is it possible to warn people before shaking occurs? When an earthquake happens, it sends out waves of energy in all directions. P-waves travel the fastest, but do not cause much shaking. S-waves are slower and can cause major shaking. Sensors in the earthquake instruments detect the faster P-waves, which arrive before the S-waves. The instruments communicate data almost instantly to an earthquake alert center, where it is determined if shaking will happen and if so, when and where. This triggers a warning message that is sent to people's phones and computers, possibly giving them several seconds to prepare for the shaking that S-waves can bring.

Doug graduated from the University of Washington with degrees in Earth and Space Sciences and History.

Continue Your Exploration

An Earthquake Warning System

This diagram shows how the waves sent out from an earthquake are detected by sensors. The sensors communicate with an alert center where an earthquake warning message is generated.

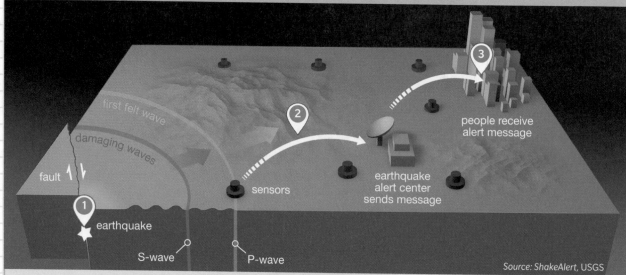

Source: ShakeAlert, USGS

① When an earthquake happens, waves of energy are sent out. Faster P-waves reach locations first. Slower S-waves follow and can cause shaking and damage.

② P-waves are detected by sensors that immediately communicate with an alert center. Here, alert messages are generated and sent to people in the area.

③ The further a person is from the earthquake source, the more warning time they will have, as the S-waves will take longer to reach them.

1. Explain why an earthquake warning system is useful even though earthquakes cannot be predicted.

2. The team at PNSN is working to make the transfer of data faster from the sensors to the alert center. Explain why this is important.

3. An earthquake warning could give people a few seconds to prepare. Apply what you've learned to provide examples of ways people could prepare for shaking.

   Transportation: stopping planes from taking off or landing

4. **Collaborate** With a partner, find another location that is prone to earthquakes. Is it near a plate boundary? Are there any warning systems in place here?

Can You Explain It?

Name: _____   Date: _____

Revisit the island that suddenly appeared off the coast of Japan.

How might this island have appeared overnight?

JAPAN

▷ Explore
ONLINE!

 EVIDENCE NOTEBOOK
Refer to the notes in your Evidence Notebook to help you construct an explanation for how this island suddenly appeared.

1. State your claim. Make sure your claim fully explains how the island could have suddenly appeared.

2. Summarize the evidence you have gathered to support your claim and explain your reasoning.

Checkpoints

Answer the following questions to check your understanding of the lesson.

Use the fossil map to answer questions 3–4.

3. This map shows four kinds of _____.
   They are now separated by a vast _____
   that they could not have crossed. Their locations
   could be explained if South America and Africa
   were _____ at the time the plants and
   animals lived.

4. In the map key, circle the fossils that serve as
   evidence that South America and Africa were
   once connected.

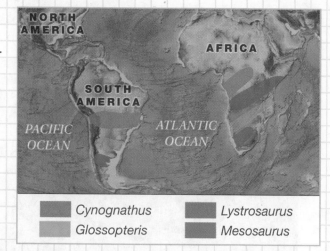

Cynognathus	Lystrosaurus
Glossopteris	Mesosaurus

---

5. Around the world, scientists have found matching fossils, landforms, and
   continental shelves. Mid-ocean ridges and trenches were discovered on
   the _____. Together these findings serve as evidence
   that Earth's surface is made up of moving _____.

Use the map showing plate boundaries to answer questions 6–7.

6. The Aleutian Trench is a deep-ocean trench that
   resulted from the sinking of the Pacific Plate
   beneath the North American Plate. These plates move
   toward / away from / past each other at a rate
   of 6–7 cm/y. Also resulting from this motion are
   mid-ocean ridges / ocean basins /
   volcanic islands.

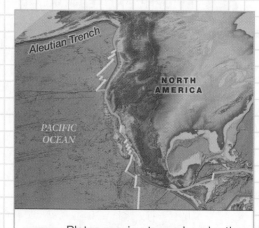

Plates moving toward each other
Plates spreading apart
Plates sliding past each other

7. Where are eruptions most likely to happen?

   A. Along the west coast of North America.

   B. Along the east coast of North America.

   C. Inland, far from any coastlines shown.

---

8. Which statements correctly describe the nature of plate motion? Circle all that apply.

   A. Energy from the sun drives plate motion.

   B. Energy from Earth's interior drives plate motion.

   C. Plates move in different directions.

   D. Most plates do not move.

Interactive Review

Complete this section to review the main concepts of the lesson.

Fossil and landform data provide evidence that continents have moved and changed.

A. How do patterns in fossil locations provide evidence that Earth's continents have moved?

At mid-ocean ridges, new rock forms. At deep-ocean trenches, rock sinks into Earth's interior. These features provide evidence that the ocean floor moves and changes.

B. Describe the different processes that occur at mid-ocean ridges and deep-ocean trenches.

Earth's outer shell is made up of tectonic plates that move in different ways. This motion forms and reshapes Earth's surface features over long time periods.

C. Provide an example of a surface feature that forms at each type of plate boundary.

The theory of plate tectonics describes how and why Earth's plates move over time.

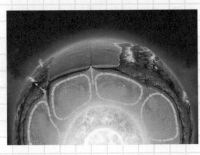

D. What causes convection currents in Earth's interior and how does it relate to plate motion?

Earth's Changing Surface

This mountain range in Banff National Park, Alberta, Canada was formed by interactions among Earth's systems.

By the end of this lesson . . .

you will be able to explain how geologic processes have shaped Earth's surface.

Go online to view the digital version of the Hands-On Lab for this lesson and to download additional lab resources.

CAN YOU EXPLAIN IT?

How has this area of the Arizona desert changed in the last 50,000 years?

Barringer Meteorite Crater was formed long ago by a meteor impact in the Arizona desert. It is named after mining engineer Daniel Moreau Barringer.

The Barringer Meteorite Crater is 1.3 km wide and extends 174 m into the Earth. The crater was formed about 50,000 years ago, when a meteorite with a mass of 300,000 metric tons hurtled through Earth's atmosphere nearly 50 times faster than a commercial jet.

1. What immediate effects might the meteorite impact have had on Earth's surface?

2. Which changes might have happened after a longer time had passed?

 EVIDENCE NOTEBOOK As you explore the lesson, gather evidence to help explain the changes to Earth's surface in this area over the last 50,000 years.

Analyzing Interactions Within the Earth System

The Earth System

Systems are used every day. A computer is one example of a system, a group of related parts that work together as a whole. In our lives, we use and interact with many systems, both human-made and natural. In fact, the Earth itself is one large system, from its core to the outer edge of its atmosphere. The **Earth system** is all the matter, energy, and processes within this boundary. The Earth system is different from the systems of other planets and moons.

There are differences between the systems of Earth and its moon.

Earth's systems interact over scales that range from microscopic to global in size.

3. What difference or differences do you see between Earth and its moon? Put a check mark to show which statements are true for Earth and for the moon.

Earth	Moon	Statements
✓		Water covers much of the surface.
		No water is visible on the surface.
		It is surrounded by air.
		The surface includes solid materials.
		Living organisms are visible on the surface.

Earth's Subsystems

The Earth system has many different parts that make up Earth's four major subsystems: the geosphere, hydrosphere, atmosphere, and biosphere. Many of Earth's materials are part of more than one subsystem. For example, fog is part of the atmosphere and the hydrosphere.

The interactions between Earth's subsystems happen over time spans from fractions of a second to billions of years. These interactions have shaped Earth's history and will determine its future.

Earth's Subsystems

Atmosphere
The atmosphere is the part of the Earth system that includes all of the gases in a layer that surrounds Earth. About 78% of the atmosphere is nitrogen. Only 21% of the atmosphere is the oxygen needed to sustain most living organisms. The last 1% of the atmosphere is composed of argon, water vapor, carbon dioxide, and other gases.

Geosphere
The geosphere is the part of the Earth system that includes all of the rocks, minerals, and landforms on Earth's surface and all the matter in Earth's interior.

Biosphere
The biosphere is the part of the Earth system that includes all living organisms, from the smallest bacterium to the largest tree.

Hydrosphere
The hydrosphere is the part of the Earth system that includes all Earth's water, whether it is on the surface, underground, or in the atmosphere. The hydrosphere includes liquid water, water vapor, and the solid water in ice and snow.

 EVIDENCE NOTEBOOK

4. Which of Earth's subsystems were affected by the meteorite impact? What changes occurred in the subsystem? Record your evidence.

5. Label each image with the appropriate subsystem. Some images may be labeled with more than one subsystem.

- geosphere
- biosphere
- atmosphere
- hydrosphere

_____

_____

_____

6. Describe how you interact with Earth's four subsystems on any given day.

The Cycling of Matter and Energy

Earth's subsystems constantly interact, and as they do, energy and matter cycle through the Earth system. Matter can be transferred as a result of interactions between the hydrosphere and the geosphere when moving water carries sediments and deposits them in a new location. Sometimes matter from outside the Earth system, such as a meteorite, becomes part of the matter in the Earth system.

Energy can be transferred by radiation from the sun, heat from Earth's interior, waves in bodies of water, and moving objects. Energy transfers from the sun and Earth's interior drive the transfer of matter between the subsystems. In fact, energy from the sun is one of the main drivers of erosion and deposition.

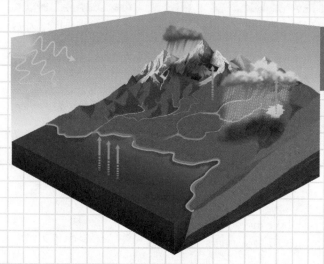

 *Explore ONLINE!*

Energy from the sun drives interactions between subsystems on Earth's surface.

7. Gravity causes rain to fall to Earth's surface. Energy from_____ causes water to _____ from the surface of the lake.

Energy from Earth's Interior

Energy from Earth's interior is transferred upward through Earth's layers, resulting in interactions among Earth's subsystems that transfer energy and matter. Hot magma in Earth's upper mantle and lower crust can eventually escape to the surface in a volcanic eruption, affecting the atmosphere, biosphere, hydrosphere, and geosphere. The eruption can cause heat and small particles of rock and minerals from deep within Earth's crust to enter the atmosphere, raising temperatures and polluting the air. The heat and matter from the eruption can also kill organisms and destroy habitats. The heat energy of the escaping lava can heat the water in streams or lakes, sometimes changing liquid water into steam. The eruption also brings minerals from within Earth to its surface, where they can be used by organisms.

Other energy transfers from Earth's interior cause the melting of rock, earthquakes, and the movement of Earth's plates.

8. The rocks that make up Earth's interior melt and form _____. Magma pushes up through the boundaries where the plates move apart.

Lava cools to form _____ on Earth's surface.

Energy from Earth's interior drives interactions between subsystems on Earth's surface.

Explain Earth's System Interactions

The interactions among Earth's subsystems are often quite complex. A single event, such as a forest fire, results in the cycling of energy and matter among the systems in many different ways. Effects on the subsystems can be positive, negative, or both.

9. **Discuss** Together with a partner, study the scene shown in the photograph. Describe subsystem interactions you can infer from the scene and explain the cycling of matter and energy that could be occurring with each interaction.

A forest fire can affect more than just the biosphere.

_____

_____

_____

_____

_____

_____

Explaining the Changes on Earth's Surface

Some changes to Earth's surface are easy to see—they are big changes that happen quickly, such as an earthquake. Other changes can start out small and occur slowly but become big changes over many, many years. An example is the erosion of Earth's mountains. The changes to Earth's surface—big or small, fast or slow—are the result of Earth's subsystems interacting.

10. **Discuss** Together with a partner, examine the photo of the alluvial fan. Was this alluvial fan formed recently, or was it formed many years ago? What evidence do you observe to support your answer?

An alluvial fan is caused by the deposition of sediment and rock by a flowing stream. This usually occurs when a stream leaves a narrow channel such as a canyon, and spreads out in a wider area, such as a plain.

Large-Scale and Small-Scale Changes

Most changes on Earth's surface are the result of interactions of Earth's subsystems. Changes on Earth's surface range from microscopic to global in scale. A smaller-scale change may be crystal formation, while ocean shore erosion is a larger-scale change. Global-sized changes, such as movements of Earth's tectonic plates, impact all of Earth.

Different Size Changes

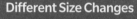
10 km

1 m

Larger-scale changes happen when the plates in Earth's crust move slowly as the mantle beneath them moves. Plate motion squeezes, stretches, and breaks Earth's crust. These motions slowly shape global-scale features such as wide ocean basins, deep-ocean trenches, and long mountain chains, like the Himalayas pictured here.

Smaller-scale changes happen when oxygen in water chemically reacts with rocks that contain iron. This reaction causes the rocks to change and break down. Similarly, plants that live on rocks, such as lichen, produce chemicals that cause rocks to break down. These changes impact much smaller areas on Earth's surface.

11. The events listed below describe changes to Earth's surface. Classify the changes as smaller-scale, medium-scale, or larger-scale by writing the correct label on the line next to each event. Assign each scale to only two events.

WORD BANK
• smaller-scale change
• medium-scale change
• larger-scale change

A. Water and ice weather and erode a rock.

smaller-scale change

B. Two plates collide, causing a mountain range to form.

C. Heavy rainfall causes a landslide.

D. An alluvial fan forms where a stream spreads out on a plain.

E. Gravity causes a rock structure on a beach to collapse into the ocean.

F. A plant dies and decays, and its nutrients become part of the soil.

EVIDENCE NOTEBOOK

12. How would you classify the size of the change to Earth's surface due to the impact of the meteorite? Provide evidence to support your answer.

Time Scale of Changes

Geologic processes happen on varying time scales. Some events that shape Earth's surface happen very quickly, such as erosion and deposition caused by floods. Other processes happen slowly over a longer period. The processes may take so long, in fact, that we may think nothing is happening. When wind, water, and ice cause erosion and deposition over a long time scale, mountains and valleys are formed. However, since these changes sometimes occur over millions and billions of years, humans usually can observe only a small part of most processes that change Earth's surface.

The same processes that shaped Earth's surface in the past continue to shape Earth's surface today. Some of these processes may have occurred more often or less often in the past than they do today. An example is the large meteorites that impacted Earth early in its history. Meteorite impacts occur much less frequently today.

Do the Math
Compare Rates of Change

Changes on Earth's surface happen at many different rates. Both rapid and slow movement can cause changes to landforms on Earth's surface. For example, when plate movement happens suddenly, it can trigger earthquakes. When plate movement happens slowly, continents can break apart and mountain ranges can form. Three changes that usually happen at different rates are:

- flow of a fast glacier (17 km/year)
- spreading at the Mid-Atlantic Ridge (2 cm/year)
- formation of a stalactite in a cave (3 mm/year)

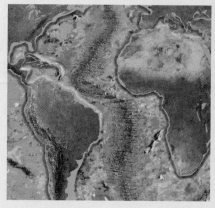

This image shows the mid-ocean ridge in the Atlantic Ocean.

---

13. In the table below, use what you know about the original rate data to complete the order column by writing slowest, middle, or fastest.

Process	Original Data	Order	Converted Data
fast glacier	17 km/year		
Mid-Atlantic Ridge	2 cm/year	middle	2 cm/year
stalactite formation	3 mm/year		

14. Complete the converted data column by converting all the rates to cm/year. Remember: 1 km = 100,000 cm and 1 cm = 10 mm

15. What is the difference between comparing the rates using the original rate data and the data converted to cm/year? Which data set is easier to use to compare the rates of change? Explain your reasoning.

16. Engineer It How could you measure the speed of a glacier if it takes a year to move several kilometers? What is one additional challenge scientists face in measuring the spreading rate at a mid-ocean ridge compared to measuring the speed of a glacier?

Fast and Slow Changes

Earth's surface has been changing over billions of years. Many of the changes happen in a matter of minutes, while others may take millions of years to occur. As you look at events that change Earth's surface, comparisons can be made to give you a sense of these time scales. For example, you can compare two events—the formation of a river delta and a river flooding—that can occur in your lifetime. A river delta forms when sediments carried by a river are deposited where it empties into the ocean. A river delta might grow slowly each day, with changes visible in a couple months or a year's time. In comparison, floods occur when there is heavy rainfall in a short period of time. This can cause lakes and rivers to overflow and flood the surrounding area. These floods can erode sediment and other materials, depositing them in new locations in a matter of hours or days.

This river delta formed from sediments deposited by the river that flows into the sea here.

The level of this river is higher than normal. It is brown due to the high level of sediment it carries.

17. A flood is a slow / fast process that has a smaller / medium / larger effect on Earth's surface.

 EVIDENCE NOTEBOOK

18. When the meteorite hit Earth, did its impact cause fast or slow changes to Earth's surface? Support your claim with evidence.

Hands-On Lab
Analyze Visual Evidence

What changes can a volcanic eruption cause? You will use maps to analyze the visible changes to the Mount St. Helens area that were caused by a powerful eruption.

MATERIALS
• colored pencils

The eruption of Mount St. Helens, a volcanic mountain in the Cascade Range located in the state of Washington, is an example of a rapid change that caused large-scale changes to Earth's surface.

The volcano had been dormant since 1857, but on the morning of May 18, 1980, a massive earthquake (5.1 on the Richter scale) caused its north side to collapse. An avalanche of rock fell onto the land below. Then gases that had been under pressure inside the mountain shot out sideways, killing 500 km² of surrounding forest. Ash rose thousands of feet into the air, and pyroclastic flows streamed down its sides. After nine hours, the eruption was over, but Earth's surface in the area was forever changed.

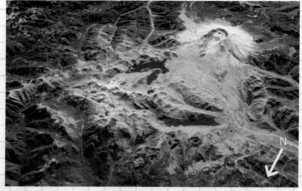

This satellite image of Mount St. Helens was taken after the eruption in 1980.

Procedure and Analysis

STEP 1 In this activity you are provided with information about Mount St. Helens and two maps of the area. One map is from the time between 1970 and 1980, before the eruption. The other map is from 1980, after the eruption.

STEP 2 Compare the two maps. Look for differences between them. What changed in the area around Mount St. Helens after the eruption?

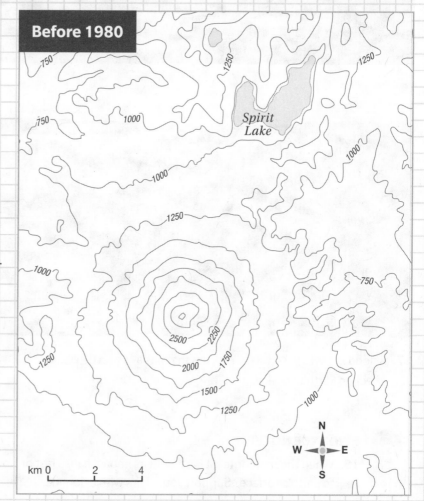

Before 1980

Spirit Lake

STEP 3 From among your observations, choose something that changed after the eruption. Use the colored pencils to indicate the feature on the "before" map and how it has changed on the "after" map. Outline or color the feature in a way that makes it clear to a viewer what you are highlighting.

STEP 4 Choose at least two other changes and mark your maps to show them.

STEP 5 Create a map legend that explains the colors and their meanings.

STEP 6 Using evidence from the maps, which statement describes Mount St. Helens after the changes occurred as a result of the eruption? Circle all that apply.

A. The shape of Spirit Lake was not affected by the eruption.

B. The land south of Mount St. Helens was changed more than the land to the north.

C. The earthquake caused the erosion and deposition of rocks and other materials.

D. The eruption left a large crater on Mount St. Helens that reduced the overall height of the mountain.

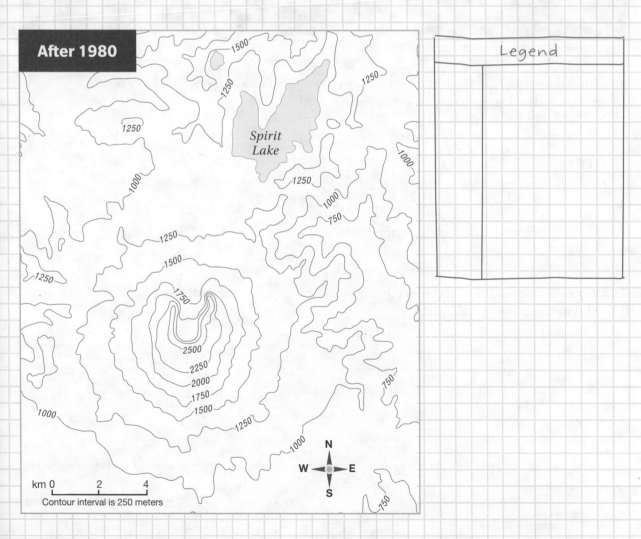

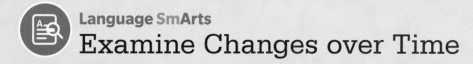
Examine Changes over Time

Earth's surface changes as a result of many processes that happen over different time and spatial scales. The interactions among Earth's subsystems can happen slowly or rapidly, and they affect Earth's surface on scales ranging from microscopic to global.

This volcanic rock has been sitting on the coastline for many years.

19. Study the photograph of the volcanic rock. Do you think the rock always looked like this? Provide evidence to support your answer.

_____

_____

_____

_____

_____

20. Write Compose a story about how the rock in the photograph came to look as it does today.

_____

_____

_____

_____

_____

_____

_____

_____

Continue Your Exploration

Name: _____   Date: _____

Check out the path below or go online to choose one of the other paths shown.

Yellowstone Is Changing

- **Hands-On Labs** 🖐
- **Destination Mars**
- **Propose Your Own Path**

Go online to choose one of these other paths.

Yellowstone National Park covers parts of Wyoming, Montana, and Idaho. About 640,000 years ago, magma in a chamber below the surface pushed Earth's crust up, creating a dome. A huge volcanic explosion emptied the magma chamber. The dome cracked and collapsed, forming the Yellowstone caldera. A caldera is a depression formed when a magma chamber below a volcano empties.

Today there is still a magma chamber below the Yellowstone caldera. In some places it is less than 10 km below the surface. About 9% of the chamber is molten rock, or magma, found in small pockets within very hot solid rock. There are also many faults, or breaks in rock, in and around the caldera. When rocks move along a fault and release energy, earthquakes occur. Many earthquakes happen near the Yellowstone caldera.

Yellowstone National Park also contains about 10,000 hydrothermal features, such as geysers and hot springs. The energy source for all these features is the magma chamber below the Yellowstone caldera. If water flows near hot rock, it can become very hot or even turn into steam. Hot springs are places where hot groundwater rises to Earth's surface. Geysers are hot springs where water and steam erupt periodically from surface pools or small vents. The geyser eruption empties an underground chamber where the water had collected. The chamber then refills with groundwater and erupts again after the water is hot enough to boil.

1. Describe an interaction between Earth's subsystems that is happening in Yellowstone National Park today. Describe the cycling of matter and flow of energy involved in this interaction.

A geyser erupts at Yellowstone National Park.

Continue Your Exploration

Cutaway Diagram of the Yellowstone Caldera Area

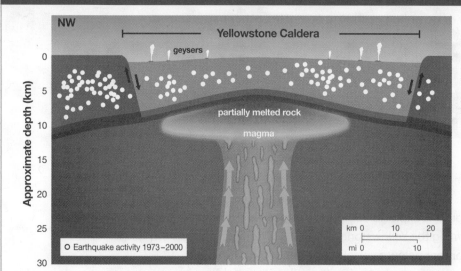

This image shows the Yellowstone caldera with rising magma pockets and geysers inside the caldera.

2. There are large faults at the edges of the Yellowstone caldera. In this diagram, these faults have arrows on either side that show the direction of movement of rock along the faults. Using what you know about earthquakes, describe where you would expect to find other faults in the rock around the Yellowstone caldera.

3. Describe the locations of the geysers in this diagram. Develop an explanation for why the geysers are found here and not in other parts of the area.

4. **Collaborate** Discuss with a classmate how Earth's surface may change in Yellowstone over the next 100 years. What features may be affected? Provide evidence from the image to support your argument.

Can You Explain It?

Name: _____   Date: _____

Revisit the crater in the Arizona desert.

How has this area of the Arizona desert changed in the last 50,000 years?

 EVIDENCE NOTEBOOK

Refer to the notes in your Evidence Notebook to help you identify the effects of the meteorite on Earth's systems as well as the changes that were observed over time.

1. State your claim. Make sure your claim fully explains how this area of the Arizona desert has changed over the last 50,000 years.

2. Summarize the evidence you have gathered to support your claim and explain your reasoning.

Checkpoints

Answer the following questions to check your understanding of the lesson.

Use the photo to answer Questions 3 and 4.

3. What factors formed the Grand Canyon? Circle all that apply.

   A. An earthquake formed the canyon.

   B. Wind eroded rock to form the canyon.

   C. The Colorado River eroded rock to form the canyon.

4. What is the primary source of energy that drove the cycling of matter that formed the Grand Canyon?

   A. the sun

   B. Earth's hot interior

   C. erosion and weathering

Use the photo to answer Questions 5 and 6.

5. This photo shows evidence of the interaction of Earth's subsystems. Which of Earth's subsystems are interacting? Circle all that apply.

   A. geosphere

   B. biosphere

   C. atmosphere

   D. hydrosphere

landslide

6. The devastation from the landslide shown—the disturbed soil, the knocked-over trees, the blocked waterway and road—are evidence that the change happened *rapidly / slowly* over time.

Interactive Review

Complete this section to review the main concepts of the lesson.

Earth's subsystems are the geosphere, atmosphere, hydrosphere, and biosphere.
Energy and matter are transferred when Earth's subsystems interact.

A. A hurricane roars through a region. Describe which of Earth's subsystems are involved in this event. Explain how these different subsystems affect one another.

Geologic processes change Earth's surface on varying scales of space and time.
They range from rapid to very slow; from large to microscopic.

B. How does the time scale of slow geologic processes affect human perception of these processes? Provide details to support your answer.

Choose one of the activities to explore how this unit connects to other topics.

☐ Physical Science Connection

Sonar and the Ocean Floor Geological features of the sea floor are as varied and interesting as land features. Scientists us *sonar*—sound navigation and ranging—as one tool to detect these geological features. Sonar technology uses sound waves to measure distances, which are recorded on an ocean floor map.

Research and make a presentation on how sonar works using sound energy and what has been discovered about the ocean floor using sonar.

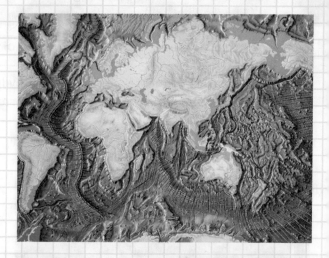

☐ Engineering Connection

Seeing the Unseen Through Data The seismograph, which detects and records the movement of seismic waves that occur in an earthquake, was invented in 1880. By the end of the 1880s, seismic stations were in place all over the world. We cannot view or travel to Earth's interior, but scientists in the late 19th century were able to determine its composition by analyzing the seismic waves recorded at different seismic stations around the world.

Research how seismologists could determine the composition of Earth's interior by analyzing the data from seismographs. Present your findings to the class.

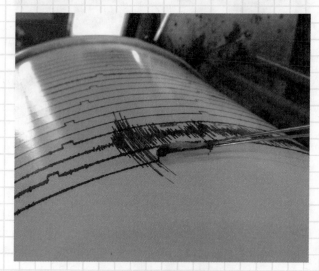

This seismogram shows the activity of waves traveling through Earth's interior during an earthquake.

☐ Art Connection

Geology and Society Geologic features play a major role in determining where people live and how human societies develop. They provide the resources that we need for our daily lives.

Research paintings that reflect geologic features and their relationships to human societies. Then, choose two paintings by different artists and make a presentation identifying each artist, the geologic feature that is portrayed in each painting, and how each painting represents the ways in which the geologic feature influences the lives of people who live near it.

Starry Night Over the Rhone by Vincent van Gogh

Name: _____   Date: _____

Use the photograph of the river delta to answer Questions 1–2.

1. At the mouth of a slow-flowing river, a broad, flat delta can form, often extending many kilometers into the sea. Which geologic processes are responsible for the formation of a river delta? Select all that apply.

   A. weathering

   B. erosion

   C. deposition

   D. plate movement

2. Which statement best describes the time and spatial scales of the formation of a delta at the mouth of a large river?

   A. rapid and local

   B. rapid and global

   C. slow and local

   D. slow and global

3. Energy from the sun and Earth's hot interior / the sun / Earth's hot interior drives the processes involved in the rock cycle.

Use the photograph to answer Question 4.

4. The tree's roots physically / chemically weather the rock, breaking the rock apart. This process is an example of an interaction between the geosphere and the atmosphere / biosphere / hydrosphere.

Name: _____ **Date:** _____

5. Complete the table by providing at least one example of how these geologic processes relate to each big concept.

Geologic Processes	Energy Source(s)	Time and Spatial Scales	Stability and Change	Patterns
Weathering, erosion, and deposition				
The rock cycle				
Tectonic plate motion				
Mountain formation				

Use the diagram to answer Questions 6–9.

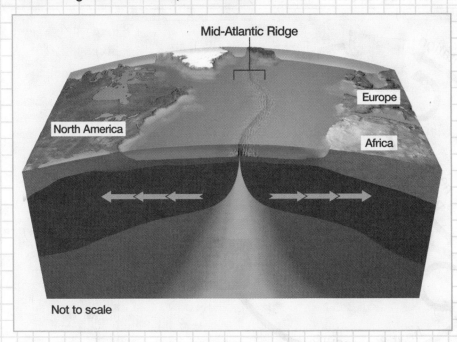

Mid-Atlantic Ridge

Europe

North America

Africa

Not to scale

6. Identify the type of plate boundary shown in this diagram and use evidence to explain your reasoning.

7. Describe at least two ways that the movement of these plates could change the Earth's surface, including a description of the time scales.

8. Iceland is an island located between North America and Europe. There are many springs where hot water comes to the surface in Iceland. Use the diagram to explain how these springs could occur.

9. The western coast of the United States has many volcanoes and frequent earthquakes. Why are these features not common along the eastern coast of the United States or the western coast of Europe?

Use the rock cycle diagram to answer Questions 10–13.

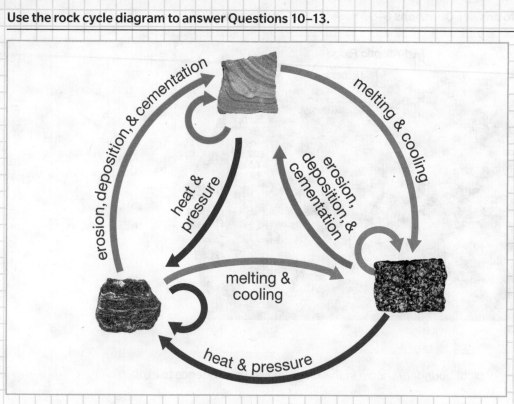

10. Based on the diagram, what changes between types of rock can occur as part of the rock cycle process?

11. What type of rock would have been formed first during Earth's history? Explain your reasoning.

12. Identify parts of the rock cycle that can only occur deep beneath the surface, and provide evidence to support your reasoning.

13. Close examination of a rock sample shows that it has many tiny fossils of seashells. Explain how you could determine whether the rock is igneous, metamorphic, or sedimentary.

Name: _____   Date: _____

What is the best location for a new bridge?

The state highway department is building a road that will directly connect the cities of Appleville and Westwood. The department has asked for local input into design decisions, and a planning committee has been formed, which includes citizens of both communities.

Two designs are being considered: a high bridge and a low bridge. Your team has been assembled to provide advice to the committee. Your job is to use the diagram below to analyze the geology of the two locations. As you develop your report, consider the criteria of the problem and constraints imposed by geology. You will then recommend a preferred location for the new bridge.

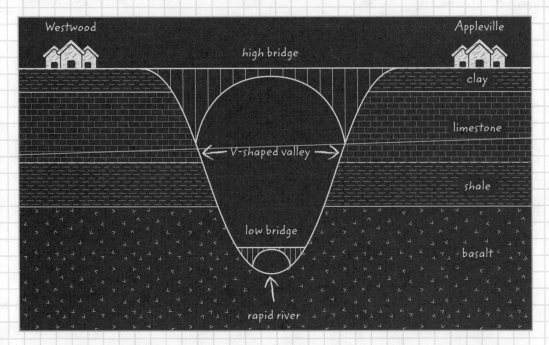

The steps below will help guide your research and develop your recommendation.

Engineer It

1. **Define the Problem** With your team, write a statement defining the problem you have been asked to solve. What are the criteria and constraints involved in determining the bridge location?

Engineer It

2. **Conduct Research** What types of geologic processes are at work in the area, and how might each process affect the area?

3. **Analyze Data** The state highway department wants the bridge to last at least 100 years. Identify how you expect these processes to change the area over the next 100 years.

4. **Identify and Recommend a Solution** Make a recommendation based on your research. Should the cities build the high bridge or low bridge? Explain your reasoning.

5. **Communicate** Present your research to the bridge committees of Appleville and Westwood. Your presentation should show the evidence of the geologic processes at work in the area and illustrate how you expect these processes to change the area over the next 100 years. Your information will help the engineers specify requirements and constraints to build a lasting bridge.

✓ **Self-Check**

	I defined the bridge location problem by identifying the criteria and the constraints.
	I researched how different geologic processes could affect conditions in the proposed locations of the bridge.
	My solution is based on evidence gathered from research and data analysis.
	My solution and recommendation was clearly communicated to others.

Earth Through Time

Lesson 1 The Age of Earth's Rocks 96

Lesson 2 Earth's History 114

Unit Review 133

Unit Performance Task 137

Paleontologists chip away at a rock face in the Madagascar Republic. They are searching for fossils of organisms that lived during earlier time periods in Earth's history.

Scientists have a systematic way to organize Earth's long history. For example, a time period called the Paleozoic era ranges from 543–251 million years ago. This era is defined by two major events in Earth's history: an explosion in plant and animal life at the beginning and a mass-extinction at the end. In this unit, you will investigate methods of determining ages of rocks and fossils, and the types of evidence that scientists use to organize Earth's history.

Why It Matters

Here are some questions to consider as you work through the unit. Can you answer any of the questions now? Revisit these questions at the end of the unit to apply what you discovered.

Questions	Notes
Why might you want to study the geologic history of a certain area? What can you learn?	
What tools and resources can you use to learn about the geologic history of an area?	
How can you use the concepts of relative dating and absolute dating to learn about the geologic history of an area?	
How might you use information from the fossil and rock records to infer what the environment of an area was like in the past?	
How might you infer what an area was like at a certain time period in Earth's history if no fossils are found in that area?	

Unit Starter: Sequencing Events

Each item on this timeline is an event from a portion of Earth's history.

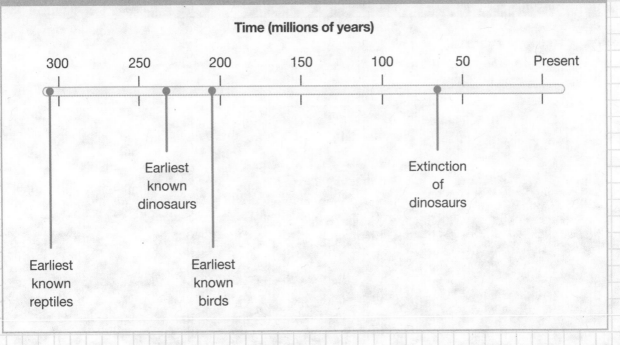

Time (millions of years)

1. This timeline spans more than *three / four* million years.

2. The earliest known dinosaurs appeared on Earth *before / after* the earliest known reptiles appeared. Dinosaurs became extinct about *45 / 65* million years ago, which was *before / after* the earliest known birds appeared.

3. When thinking about Earth's history, it is important to remember that events that occurred millions of years ago occurred *before / after* events that took place thousands of years ago.

▷ Go online to download the Unit Project Worksheet to help you plan your project.

Unit Project

Paleogeography

Become a paleontologist and research the geologic history of a state, country, or geographic region. Use information based on the types and ages of rocks found, fossil data, and geologic features to tell a story about the area's geologic past.

The Age of Earth's Rocks

The colorful rock layers that make up these hills in Oregon contain clues about the history of the area.

By the end of this lesson . . .

you will be able to explain how scientists determine the ages of Earth's rocks and fossils.

CAN YOU EXPLAIN IT?

How could the ages of these dinosaurs be determined?

History of Dinosaur Provincial Park

77–75 million years ago
These dinosaurs lived alongside turtles, crocodiles, and small mammals. The area consisted of swamps and lush vegetation, as well as many rivers that flowed into a nearby sea.

75–72 million years ago
The nearby sea rose slowly for a few million years until it completely covered the area. This sea was full of creatures including sharks and the animals shown in this drawing.

Present Day
Over the last 72 million years, this area and its plants and animals changed many times. This is a photo of the area today, now known as Dinosaur Provincial Park. The park is in Alberta, Canada.

1. The rocks and fossils found today in Dinosaur Provincial Park tell us about the park's past environments, plants, and animals. In order to know *when* each plant or animal existed, one would need to know the ages of the fossils. How do you think the ages of these fossils were determined?

 EVIDENCE NOTEBOOK As you explore this lesson, gather evidence to help explain how the ages of fossils are determined.

Describing the Formation of Sedimentary Rocks and Fossils

Why would anyone want to study rocks? Rocks tell us a lot about the past. Earth's rocks range from hundreds to billions of years old! Many of the rocks you see existed before humans, and even before many of the plants or animals that you see lived on Earth.

Earth is ever-changing. Although rocks seem like they are permanent, the rocks you see today were not always there. Rocks form and change as processes such as erosion, deposition, melting, and burial take place over thousands to millions of years. Different rocks form in different environments. For example, granite is an igneous rock that forms when magma cools beneath Earth's surface. Basalt is an igneous rock that forms when lava cools above Earth's surface. Limestone and siltstone are sedimentary rocks that can form in bodies of water as materials settle in layers and harden over time.

2. **Discuss** With a classmate, look at the rock layers in the picture. Note any patterns in their ages. Which rock layer formed first?

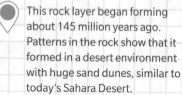 This rock layer began forming about 145 million years ago. Patterns in the rock show that it formed in a desert environment with huge sand dunes, similar to today's Sahara Desert.

This rock layer formed about 200 million years ago. By studying this rock layer, scientists can tell it formed where tropical lakes and streams once existed.

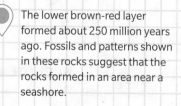 The lower brown-red layer formed about 250 million years ago. Fossils and patterns shown in these rocks suggest that the rocks formed in an area near a seashore.

Sedimentary Rock Formation

Sedimentary rocks are made of tiny rock pieces called *sediment*. Some sedimentary rocks are made from the remains of plants and animals. For example, limestone can be made of bits of shells.

Sedimentary rock formation begins when erosion moves sediment to low-lying areas such as valleys and lake bottoms. The sediment settles in layers and becomes compressed as lower layers are buried under the weight of upper layers. Water containing dissolved substances seeps into the sediment layers. The substances come out of the solution and harden, acting as a glue to form a rock layer.

As sedimentary layers form, they stack up one by one. If undisturbed by Earth processes, sedimentary rocks stay in horizontal layers. The oldest layer is at the bottom and the youngest layer is at the top.

Fossils in Sedimentary Rock

When a plant or animal dies, it often decomposes or is eaten by animals. However, if it is quickly buried by sediment, evidence of the organism can be preserved. The sediment hardens and becomes a rock, which now contains a fossil. *Fossils* are the traces or remains of an organism that lived long ago.

Fossils are most commonly preserved in sedimentary rock. Some fossils look like parts of an organism but are not the organism's actual parts. Bone, shell, or wood, for example, can be replaced by minerals that form a rock version of the part. Fossils can also show traces of an animal's activity, such as footprints or burrows. Not all fossils are preserved in rock. Ice, tar, and tree sap can contain fossils as well.

Over time, shells and sediment pile up at the bottom of lakes and oceans. These pieces can form rocks such as limestone.

Over very long periods, bodies of water can dry up. As the water evaporates, dissolved substances in the water become solids. This can form sedimentary rock layers such as gypsum.

After hundreds to thousands of years, sediment and parts from shelled animals that lived in the past may be compressed and cemented into rocks like this limestone.

3. Engineer It You want to explore rock layers in a region to find fossils and clues about the past. There is one problem: there are no exposed cliffs or areas where you can see the rock layers. They are all below the ground. Propose a solution to this problem. Can you think of any helpful tools or technology?

4. Under certain conditions, dead organisms can be preserved as fossils. Write captions for the second and third photos below to tell how the living starfish became a fossil.

Different types of starfish have lived on Earth for over 400 million years! The starfish in this photo lives in a coral reef in the ocean.

Analyze Fossils to Describe Earth's Past

Fossils provide evidence about past life and environments. For example, fossils of corals and starfish indicate that a marine environment once existed in the area where the fossils were found.

5. Look at each image. Use the words from the word bank to label each fossil with the name of the environment in which it likely formed.

WORD BANK
• a tropical forest
• a lake
• a grassland

A. _____   B. _____   C. _____

Determining the Relative Ages of Rocks

Relative Age

Rocks and fossils tell us a lot about Earth's past environments and organisms. Some rocks even tell us about events such as meteorite impacts and volcanic eruptions. But how can rocks and fossils tell us when events like these happened? One way is by determining the relative ages of rocks. *Relative age* is the age of something relative to something else. For example, one friend might be older than you. Your other friend might be younger than you. These are descriptions of your friends' relative ages. You can describe relative age without knowing actual age.

Taral made pancakes for his friends. He cooked the pancakes one at a time while stacking them on a plate.

6. **Discuss** Think about the relative ages of these pancakes. Can you explain which is the oldest and which is the youngest?

Hands-On Lab
Model Rock Layers to Determine Relative Age

How can building a model help you determine the order in which rocks form? A physical model can help you see how a sequence of rocks can form over time, one by one. It can also help you make observations about the rocks' relative ages.

In the real world, rock sequences can span over large areas. Often, rocks are not visible because they are beneath Earth's surface, but sometimes they are exposed along cliffs or where a hill was cut through for road construction.

Procedure

STEP 1 Discuss Gather your materials. Discuss with a group or partner how you can use your materials to make a model of four sedimentary rock layers.

STEP 2 Choose four rocks from the list. Note the environment in which each type of rock formed. This is also known as a rock's depositional environment.

- **Sandstone with fossils** formed in a sandy ocean bottom (yellow clay with fossil materials)
- **Shale** formed in a deep, muddy lake (brown clay)
- **Siltstone** formed in a river floodplain (red clay)
- **Sandstone** formed in a sandy desert (yellow clay)
- **Coal** formed in a tropical swamp (black clay)
- **Limestone** formed in a shallow sea (white clay)

STEP 3 Build your model. Starting at the bottom of the table, complete rows 1–4 with the information listed above about each of your rock layers.

Order of Events	Rock type	Depositional environment	Material used
5. Fifth			
4. Fourth			
3. Third			
2. Second			
1. First			

STEP 4 Choose one of these events to model in your set of rock layers. Be sure to add the event to the table in the top row. Use the plastic knife or another color of clay to represent the chosen event.

- **Igneous intrusion:** Magma rose and intruded through some of the sedimentary rock layers. The magma cooled into igneous rock.

- **Lava flow:** Magma intruded through all rock layers making its way to the surface (where it is then called lava). The lava flowed over the top of the existing rock layers and cooled into a new layer of igneous rock.

- **Fault:** Forces within Earth can move pieces of the ground and cause a crack to form. This is called a *fault*. Rocks are shifted up or down along faults.

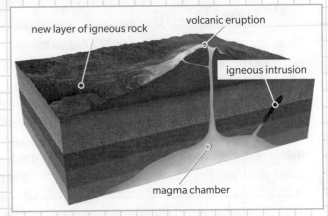

This diagram shows both an igneous intrusion below Earth's surface and a lava flow on Earth's surface.

Forces deep within Earth can form a fault where rocks shift up or down.

Analysis

STEP 5 **Language SmArts** Use your table and knowledge of relative age to write a short informative paragraph that explains how your model represents environmental changes in an area over time.

STEP 6 **Draw** Exchange models with another group. Analyze the other group's model to determine the order in which each rock formed. Make a sketch of the model and label it to show the relative ages of the rocks and the event. When you are done, exchange information with the other group to check if you correctly sequenced the layers and features.

Relative Dating

Think about the stack of pancakes. The oldest pancake is the one that was made first and placed at the bottom of the stack. The last pancake made ended up on top of the stack. It is the youngest. This is like a stack of sedimentary rock layers; the oldest layer is at the bottom and the youngest is at the top. This is true as long as rock layers are undisturbed. That is, the rock layers have not been greatly deformed by geologic processes.

When you determined the relative ages of the pancakes, you used relative dating. **Relative dating** is any method of determining whether something is older or younger than something else. Geologists use relative dating to determine the relative ages of rocks, fossils, and features such as faults. What if you cut the stack of pancakes in half? The cut happened after the pancakes were made, so the cut is younger than the pancakes. The same is true for a fault or an igneous intrusion that cuts across rock layers. That is, the feature is younger than the rocks it cuts across.

Scientists find the relative ages of rocks to compile the rock record. The *rock record* is all of Earth's known rocks and the information they contain. The rock record allows scientists to piece together some of Earth's past environments and events.

igneous intrusion

7. Magma intruded into these sedimentary rocks, cooled, and formed a diagonal band of igneous rock. The intrusion is older / younger than the sedimentary rocks.

Fossils

A fossil is the same age as the rock in which it is found, because the rock and the fossil formed at the same time. Therefore, in undisturbed sedimentary rock layers, the youngest fossils are at the top and the oldest are at the bottom. An *index fossil* is the remains of a plant or animal that was common, widespread, and lived over a relatively short period of time, such as 1 million years or less. If two different rocks contain the same index fossil, one can conclude that those rocks are of a similar age. Both rocks must have formed during the time in which that plant or animal lived on Earth.

Scientists have collected and compared the relative ages of fossils all around the world. This gives us a picture of how life on Earth has changed over its long history. The full set of all known fossils, and the information learned from these fossils, is called the *fossil record*. As more fossils are discovered, the fossil record grows and we learn more about when Earth's ancient plants and animals lived.

 EVIDENCE NOTEBOOK

8. How could the rock and fossils records help provide information about the dinosaurs from the beginning of this lesson?

9. This type of trilobite is an index fossil that lived about 440 million years ago. Fossils of the trilobite and the brittle star were found in the same rock layer. What can you infer about these two organisms?

   A. They must have lived at the same time.

   B. They must have been closely related.

   C. They must have lived in different habitats.

   D. They must be younger than the rock layer.

Unconformities

Some rock layers are missing, forming gaps in the rock record. Such a gap is called an *unconformity*. These gaps can occur when rock layers are eroded or when sediment is not deposited for a period of time. In this way, rock layers are like pages in a book of Earth's history—only some pages were torn out or never written in the first place!

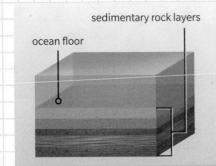
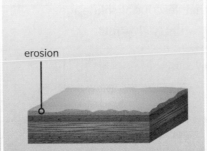
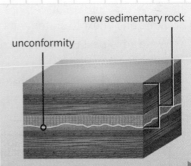

Over millions of years, sediment settles on the seafloor, forming rock layers.

Sea level drops and exposes the rocks. Some rock layers are eroded away.

New rock layers form over the old set of layers—an unconformity now exists.

Determine Relative Age

The locations of rock layers, fossils, faults, and intrusions can be used to determine their relative ages. Scientists use relative dating to piece together Earth's history. Look at the rock layers and features in the diagram.

10. Number the diagram to show the relative ages of the rocks and features. Use the number 1 for the first (oldest) rock layer or feature. Use the number 7 for the most recent (youngest) rock layer or feature.

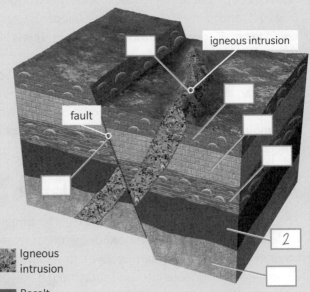

 Sandstone   Limestone   Igneous intrusion

 Shale with fossils   Limestone with fossils   Basalt

Using Absolute and Relative Age

Absolute Age

Relative age is a comparison that gives the age of one thing compared to the age of another thing. *Absolute age* is the age of an object expressed in units of time. In other words, absolute age is the actual age of something.

11. Discuss How do you think scientists figured out the absolute age of this zircon mineral?

This tiny black speck is a mineral that was found in a sandstone rock in Australia. It's about 4.2 billion years old. The person holding it is Simon Wilde, who discovered it in 1984.

12. Write an A next to statements that describe absolute age. Write an R next to those that describe relative age.

R	I am younger than my cousin.
	I am 14 years old.
	That is the oldest bicycle I've ever seen.

	My cat lived to be 15 years old.
	This coin is the newest in my collection.
	This is the last book in the series.

Absolute Dating

In the 1950s, technology made it possible to find the absolute ages of some rocks. **Absolute dating** is any method of measuring the actual age of something in years. Absolute dating works for igneous rocks, which originate from hot liquid magma or lava that cools and hardens. As soon as this happens, unstable particles in the igneous rock begin to break down into a more stable form. This is like beginning a countdown, since there is a limited amount of unstable material.

There are different types of unstable particles. Some break down in seconds. Others can take millions of years to change. The rates of change for these different particles are known and used in an equation to find a rock's age. To solve this equation, the amounts of unstable and stable particles in a rock must also be known. These amounts are measured by analyzing a sample of the rock in a laboratory.

Absolute Dating and Relative Dating

Absolute dating and relative dating are used together to provide a more complete understanding of Earth's history. Knowing the absolute age of an igneous rock next to other rock layers helps to narrow down the relative ages of the other rock layers. For example, say an igneous intrusion cuts through a layer of sandstone. Absolute dating shows that the igneous rock is 20 million years old. That means the sandstone is older than 20 million years. The sandstone existed before the intrusion occurred.

![Do the Math icon]

Do the Math
Determine Absolute Age

To find the absolute age of a rock, the rate at which the unstable particles change must be known. *Half-life* is the amount of time needed for half of the unstable particles to change into stable ones. Many types of unstable particles can be found in rocks, and each has a different half-life.

    The igneous rock shown formed when magma from Earth's interior traveled to the surface and cooled. The rock contains unstable particles of uranium that break down into a more stable form of lead over time. The rate at which the uranium breaks down is known. It takes 704 million years for half the rock's uranium to change to lead. That is, the half-life is 704 million years. At any point in time, the amounts of uranium and lead can be measured to find the rock's age.

$A = n \times h$

A = Age of rock
n = number of half-lives passed
h = half-life of unstable particle

The Breakdown of Uranium to Lead over Three Half Lives

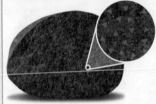   

 Uranium Lead

Igneous rock forms This igneous rock just formed. It contains unstable uranium particles. At this time, none of the uranium has changed into lead.

704 million years later One half-life has passed. Half of the unstable uranium has changed into a more stable form of lead. The rock is 704 million years old.

Another 704 million years later Another half-life has passed, so half of the remaining uranium has changed into lead. The rock is now 1,408 million years old.

Another 704 million years later The pattern continues. For every half-life, half of the remaining uranium changes to lead.

13. Fill in the table as you explore the half-life diagram.

Half-Lives Passed	Unstable Particles in the Rock	Stable Form of the Particle	Time Passed (Millions of Years)
0	16	0	0
1	8	8	704
2	4	12	1408
3		14	

EVIDENCE NOTEBOOK

14. Think back to the dinosaurs in Dinosaur Provincial Park. Could relative dating or absolute dating be used to determine the ages of these fossils? Explain.

The Absolute Age of Earth

Absolute dating can be used to find the age of Earth, but not by using rocks from Earth. This is because the first rocks that formed on Earth have been eroded, melted, or buried under younger rocks long ago. Therefore, most rocks on Earth are younger than Earth itself—with one exception: meteorites.

Meteorites are small, rocky bodies that have traveled through space and fallen to Earth's surface. The absolute ages of meteorites can be determined. Because Earth formed at the same time as other bodies in our solar system, meteorites should be the same age as Earth. Absolute dating of meteorites and moon rocks suggest that Earth is about 4.6 billion years old.

15. Recall the zircon mineral found in the sandstone in Australia. The zircon formed long before the sandstone. It was part of an igneous rock before it became part of the sandstone. Complete each statement to make it true.

_____ dating was used to determine the age of the sandstone rock compared to the ages of the rocks around it. _____ dating was used to calculate the actual age of the zircon mineral.

Use Relative and Absolute Dating Together

Scientists use both relative and absolute dating to find the ages of rocks and fossils. A field geologist sketched these rocks to help determine their ages.

16. What can you conclude based on the absolute ages of the igneous rocks given? Check the statement(s) that you believe to be true:

_____ The shale with fossils is also 175 million years old.

_____ The limestone is between 200 and 175 million years old.

_____ The sandstone must be less than 200 million years old.

_____ The rocks shifted along the fault less than 175 million years ago.

175 million years

200 million years

Sandstone   Limestone   Igneous intrusion

Shale with fossils   Limestone with fossils   Basalt

Continue Your Exploration

Name: _____   Date: _____

Check out the path below or go online to choose one of the other paths shown.

Exploring the Ashfall Fossil Beds

- Hands-on Labs
- Exploring Local Geology
- Propose Your Own Path

Go online to choose one of these other paths.

Although most fossils are preserved by sedimentary rock, some are preserved by igneous rock. Look at these fossils of ancient animals from the Ashfall Fossil Beds in Nebraska. The animals were killed by hot volcanic ash that covered the area during an eruption. As the ash settled into thick layers, it cooled and hardened into rock. Volcanic ash can fall from the sky or flow downhill during an eruption. Ash flows can burn everything in their path, but sometimes they will preserve animals such as these.

These rocks contain fossils of rhinos and stallions that died in a volcanic ash flow.

- young adult male rhino "Tusker"
- large 3-toed stallion "Cormo"
- adult female rhino "Sandy" with baby "Justin"
- rhino calf
- rhino calves (possibly twins) "T.L." and "R.G.C."

Continue Your Exploration

The following field notes were recorded in the area:

Date: October 9
Location: Ashfall Fossil Beds State Historical Park, Nebraska
Observations and Notes:

- The fossils in the photo were uncovered in the Ashfall Fossil Beds layer.
- Other fossils exist above and below the Ashfall Fossil Beds as shown in the table.
- The Ashfall Fossil Beds are as thick as three meters in some places.
- Absolute dating shows that the Ashfall Fossil Beds formed 12 million years ago.

Rocks and Fossils from the Ashfall Fossil Beds State Historical Park	
Rock Layers	**Fossils Found**
Loose sand and gravel	zebras, lemmings, giant camels, muskrats, giant beavers
Sandstone layer	barrel-bodied rhinos, giant land tortoises, camels, rodents, horses
Ashfall Fossil Beds layer	
Sandstone layer	
Sandy and silty sedimentary rock layers	alligators, fish, hornless rhinos, giant salamanders

1. The ash layer is igneous rock. Absolute dating shows the ash layer is 12 million years old. What can you infer about the animals found in the ash layer?

2. **Language SmArts** Write a short informative report applying what you've learned to explain the history of the area.

- Use the observations and notes to tell what happened in the area over time.
- How old are the fossils in the ash layer? What was the area like before this?
- How can absolute and relative dating help you explain how the area changed?

3. **Collaborate** Many articles about the Ashfall Fossil Beds are available in magazines and on the Internet. Find several articles. In a group discussion, cite specific evidence that could help you identify the article that provides the most accurate and thorough information. Discuss the evidence with the group and try to come to an agreement about which article to select.

Can You Explain It?

Name: _____ **Date:** _____

Revisit the dinosaurs from Dinosaur Provincial Park in Alberta, Canada.

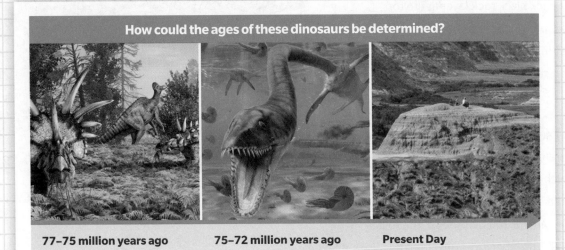

How could the ages of these dinosaurs be determined?

| 77–75 million years ago | 75–72 million years ago | Present Day |

 EVIDENCE NOTEBOOK

Refer to the notes in your Evidence Notebook to help you construct an explanation for how the ages of fossils are determined.

1. State your claim. Make sure your claim fully explains how the ages of the dinosaur fossils found in Dinosaur Provincial Park could be determined.

2. Summarize the evidence you have gathered to support your claim and explain your reasoning.

Checkpoints

Use the photo to answer Questions 3 and 4.

3. Which rock layer or feature of the cliff formed most recently?

   A. the thick black rock layer at the top

   B. the fault running through the center

   C. the white rock layer near the bottom

   D. the gray rock layer at the very bottom

4. Which of the following questions could be answered from the information in the photo? Choose all that apply.

   A. Which is the oldest rock layer?

   B. When did the oldest rock layer form?

   C. What are the relative ages of the rocks?

   D. What is the absolute age of the most recent layer?

   E. What year did the earthquake happen that caused the fault?

Use the diagram of undisturbed rock layers and features to answer Questions 5 and 6.

5. Which of the following statements are true? Choose all that apply.

   A. All fossils are over 175 million years old.

   B. The fault shifted the rocks more than 175 million years ago.

   C. All fossils formed between 175 and 200 million years ago.

   D. The sandstone is older than 200 million years old.

   E. The sandstone is younger than 200 million years old.

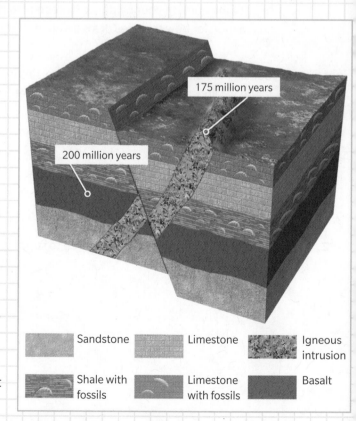

6. Circle the correct term to complete each statement.

   The igneous intrusion is younger / older than the fault.

   The fossils found in the shale are from animals that lived before / after the animals that formed fossils in the limestone.

Interactive Review

Complete this interactive study guide to review the lesson.

Sedimentary rock layers—and the fossils in those rock layers—help us to understand Earth's history.

A. Summarize how sedimentary rock and fossils form.

Geologists use relative dating to compare the ages of different rock layers and the fossils in those layers.

B. A student makes a sandwich with several layers of bread and cheese. Then the student cuts the sandwich and says it models how a fault cut through rock layers after the rock layers formed. Explain how the example of the sandwich relates to relative dating.

The combination of absolute and relative dating allows scientists to determine the ages of rocks and fossils. Absolute dating provides evidence that helps us estimate the age of Earth.

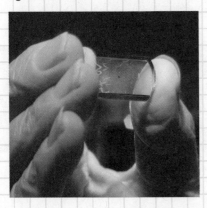

C. How can scientists find the absolute ages of igneous rocks?

Earth's History

This fossil of a tyrannosaur skeleton was found buried in a layer of sandstone, a sedimentary rock.

By the end of this lesson . . .

you will be able to explain how evidence is used to organize Earth's history into the geologic time scale.

CAN YOU EXPLAIN IT?

What evidence is used to construct this timeline of Earth's history?

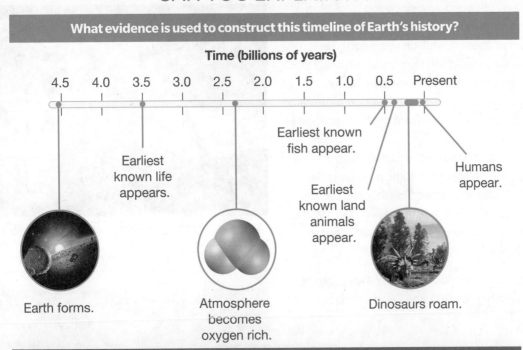

Time (billions of years)

4.5 4.0 3.5 3.0 2.5 2.0 1.5 1.0 0.5 Present

Earliest known life appears.

Earliest known fish appear.

Earliest known land animals appear.

Humans appear.

Earth forms.

Atmosphere becomes oxygen rich.

Dinosaurs roam.

There is a growing body of evidence showing that the first known life forms appeared at least 3.5 billion years ago. Complex life did not evolve until more than a billion years later, and the first humans showed up only 200,000 years ago.

1. Review this geologic timeline of events in Earth's history. What kinds of evidence are used to make timelines like this one?

EVIDENCE NOTEBOOK As you explore the lesson, gather evidence to help you explain what kinds of evidence are used to construct geologic time scales.

Describing Geologic Change

You have likely changed a lot since you were born. Just imagine all the changes Earth has been through since it formed about 4.6 billion years ago! Geologic processes such as weathering, erosion, and tectonic plate motion constantly reshape Earth. Many landforms you see today—such as rugged mountains and steep canyons—formed from geologic processes over millions of years.

To learn about changes in Earth's past, we can look to the present. Many geologic processes that shape Earth today also shaped Earth in the past. For example, volcanoes erupted, glaciers carved valleys, and sediment was deposited to form sedimentary rock. These processes still happen today.

2. **Discuss** Analyze the two photos. Describe the rate at which glaciers shape Earth's surface.

Glaciers are like slow-moving rivers of ice that scrape over land, picking up and moving rock. This glacier has been inching its way down this valley for thousands of years.

After valley glaciers melt, wide U-shaped valleys such as this one are left behind.

The Rate of Geologic Change

Most geologic processes change Earth's surface so slowly that you would not notice a difference in your lifetime. But over thousands to millions of years, geologic processes cause major changes to landscapes. For example, weathering and erosion are wearing down the Appalachian Mountains by about 6 meters (m) every million years. Over time, the rugged peaks have become rolling hills. The movement of tectonic plates is another example—they move at a rate of a few centimeters each year. Yet over millions of years, this motion builds tall mountain ranges and forms entire ocean basins.

Not all geologic change is slow. Some processes can alter large areas or the whole planet within a short period. An example is the meteorite that struck the Yucatan Peninsula in Mexico about 65 million years ago. It sent debris into the atmosphere that blocked sunlight for years and likely contributed to a mass extinction.

The frequency of meteorite impacts, volcanic eruptions, and widespread glaciation have varied during different periods of Earth's history. Scientists take this information into account when they attempt to reconstruct Earth's geologic past.

3. Geologic change is shown in each photo. Read each description, and then label the images to tell whether you think that the change is relatively *fast* or *slow*.

For millions of years, two tectonic plates have been pushing up the Himalayan Mountains. They are still growing today at about 1 centimeter per year.

The Colorado River has been carving a path through the Grand Canyon for at least 5 million years. In some spots, the canyon is 1620 meters (m) deep and continues to get deeper today.

This landslide was caused when the force of gravity suddenly triggered the movement of rocks and soil down the slope of this mountain.

Do the Math
Describe Scales of Time

How long is one million years? It helps to think about this in terms of numbers that are more familiar to us. For example, how many human lifetimes are in one million years?

STEP 1 Assume the average human lifetime is 80 years. The question asks how many human lifetimes are in 1 million years, so we need to find out how many times 80 divides into 1,000,000.

STEP 2 $\frac{1,000,000}{80} = 12,500$

There are 12,500 human lifetimes in one million years.

4. The Himalayan Mountains have been growing slowly for about 50 million years. Using the same method, find out how many human lifetimes have passed since the Himalayan Mountains began to grow.

STEP 1

STEP 2

Explaining Evidence of Earth's Past

Scientists analyze Earth's rocks and fossils to piece together Earth's past. Rocks and fossils contain clues that tell how they formed. They also can tell us about the past conditions or environments in which they formed. For example, *shale* is a sedimentary rock that forms at the bottoms of lakes and other bodies of water. *Tuff* is a rock that forms from the settling of ash from volcanic eruptions.

These layers of volcanic tuff in California formed as volcanic ash settled and cooled. Some of the ash shown here traveled all the way from Wyoming from a supervolcano eruption! This eruption spread over 1,000 cubic kilometers of ash over the United States.

5. Absolute dating shows that the volcanic tuff from the Wyoming eruption is 630,000 years old. How long ago did the supervolcano eruption occur?

Rocks Give Clues about Earth's Past

Rocks are like the pages of a book about Earth's past. Rocks contain information about past conditions and environments, such as whether an area was covered in swamps or glaciers. Rocks also tell us about past processes and events, such as floods and eruptions. A series of rocks from one place can be ordered to find the order in which certain environments existed or when certain events took place. This is done using relative and absolute dating techniques. Around the world, geologists collaborate and share information about rocks. The *rock record* is all of Earth's known rocks.

6. The rocks in the first row of photos give clues about how they formed. The photos in the second row show different environments. Match the rocks in the first row to the type of environment they likely formed in by writing A, B, or C in the correct box.

This dark layer of rock is called *coal*. Coal formation begins with the decay of plants in tropical swamps and the entire process can take millions of years.

Rocks are worn down as they are tumbled along river bottoms. Over time, they can be cemented together to form a new rock called *conglomerate*.

This landscape is covered by an igneous rock called *basalt*. The basalt formed as lava flows poured over the land and cooled into rock.

A

B

C

Fossils Give Clues about Earth's Past

In addition to rocks, scientists study fossils to find out about Earth's past. Scientists around the world share fossil information to better understand the history of life on Earth. The *fossil record* is a record of all of Earth's known fossils.

A fossil's age can be determined by the age of the rock layer in which it was found. If a fossil is found in a rock layer of an unknown age, scientists check to see if the same fossil is found in any other rock of a known age. When ordered from oldest to youngest, fossils show how life has changed over time. Along with the rocks they are found in, fossils give clues about Earth's past environments. For example, the teeth of a 10-meter (m) long shark were found in a rock layer in Kansas and determined to be about 89 million years old. This indicates that a sea covered this part of Kansas about 89 million years ago.

 EVIDENCE NOTEBOOK

7. How do rocks and fossils tell us about events and conditions from Earth's past? Record your evidence.

Analysis of Rock Layers

8. A field geologist conducted a study of an undisturbed sequence of rocks. She made a sketch, took photos, and researched information about each rock. Complete the notes below to help her construct an explanation of what happened over time in this area.

Research Notes This igneous rock formed as volcanic eruptions poured lava over the area. According to absolute dating, the rock is about 50 million years old.

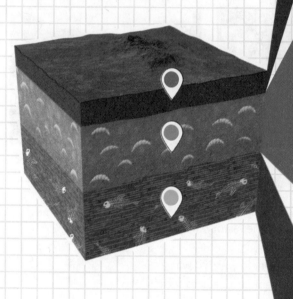

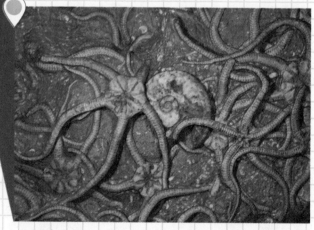

Research Notes This sandstone formed as sand was deposited in layers on a seashore. Scientists found fossils of crocodiles and turtles in exposed portions of the rock layers.

This area was first covered by a deep sea. Over a long period of time, the sea level lowered until a shoreline was left. After the sea completely dried up,

_____

_____

_____

_____

_____

_____

_____

Research Notes This shale formed from sediment that built up at the bottom of an ancient sea. Found in the shale are brittle stars that lived 188 million years ago.

Correlate Rock Sequences

Three scientists conducted an investigation in a region to learn about the plants and animals that had lived there in the past. Each scientist studied a different area in the region and made a sketch of the rock layers and fossils in that area. They compiled their sketches into a single diagram to compare the rocks and fossils found across the region.

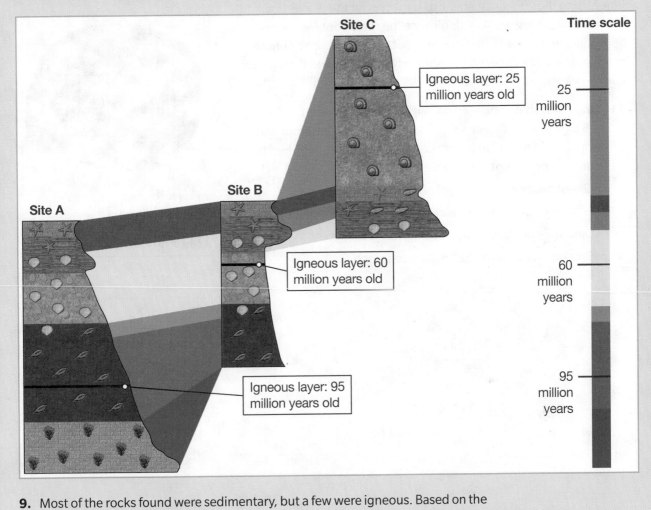

9. Most of the rocks found were sedimentary, but a few were igneous. Based on the absolute ages of the igneous rocks, help the scientists describe the relative ages of the fossils by writing either *younger* or *older*.

   The blue sea lily fossils are in the bottom rock layer, below the 95-million-year-old igneous rock layer. Therefore, the sea lilies lived over 95 million years ago. The green leaves are _____ than the sea lilies. The yellow clams are _____ than the green leaves, but they are _____ than the orange mollusks and red starfish. The youngest fossils are the purple oysters.

10. Name any plants or animals that existed during the following times:

   A. _____
      existed between 95 and 60 million years ago.

   B. _____
      existed between 60 and 25 million years ago.

   C. _____
      existed after 25 million years ago.

Describing Evidence for the Geologic Time Scale

How do the rock and fossil records provide evidence of change over time? Using these records, scientists can construct timelines that describe Earth's history. A geologic timeline can be detailed or general. Some timelines show geologic events, such as ice ages and periods of volcanic activity. Others focus on how life has changed throughout Earth's history.

11. **Draw** A lot has happened on Earth over the course of 4.6 billion years. Create a timeline that shows at least four items from Earth's past. Can you make your timeline to scale? Feel free to add your own events, or choose from the list.

    • Oldest mineral—4 billion years old

    • First flowering plants appear—145 million years ago

    • Dinosaurs become extinct—65 million years ago

    • Breakup of Pangaea—220 million years ago

This insect trapped in 45-million-year-old amber is part of the fossil record.

Earth has existed for about 4.6 billion years. The **geologic time scale** is used to organize Earth's long history into manageable parts. The geologic time scale is continually updated as new rock and fossil evidence is discovered.

The further we go back in time, the less rock and fossil information we have. This is because Earth's oldest rocks have undergone great changes over the past few billion years. Many of the oldest rocks have either been buried deep below the surface or they have melted in Earth's hot interior.

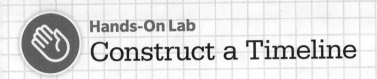

Hands-On Lab
Construct a Timeline

How could you construct a timeline of different events from your life and the lives of others in a group? Absolute dating and relative dating can help you build a model that organizes events in order.

Procedure and Analysis

STEP 1 Gather two objects that represent two events in your life. Label one object with an absolute date. For example, you may have a photo of a vacation labeled "Arizona Vacation, March 2011." Label the second object with a relative date that is based on the absolute date of the first object. For example, your second object might be a favorite book given to you after your vacation, labeled "Book given after Arizona Vacation, March 2011."

STEP 2 In your group, display your labeled objects in a central area. Collaborate with your classmates to try to arrange everything from oldest to most recent. You may want to make a chart to help you organize the events.

STEP 3 Identify any gaps or difficulties you have in your timeline, particularly with events that have relative dates. Ask questions about one another's events and use the answers to finalize the timeline.

STEP 4 What methods did you use to sequence the events? Were you able to sequence all the events in proper chronological order? Why or why not?

STEP 5 How does this activity relate to the rock record (or the fossil record)?

STEP 6 **Engineer It** Think about models that show events over time. Why would scale be important when developing these models? Explain steps that scientists can take to make a scale model of events that happen over time.

The Geologic Time Scale

Earth's entire history is divided into four major eons, shown in the top row of the diagram. In the second row, the three eras within the Phanerozoic eon are shown. Within each era are several periods, and within each period are even smaller divisions of time called epochs. Currently, we live in the Holocene epoch of the Quaternary period, which is part of the Cenozoic era and the Phanerozoic eon.

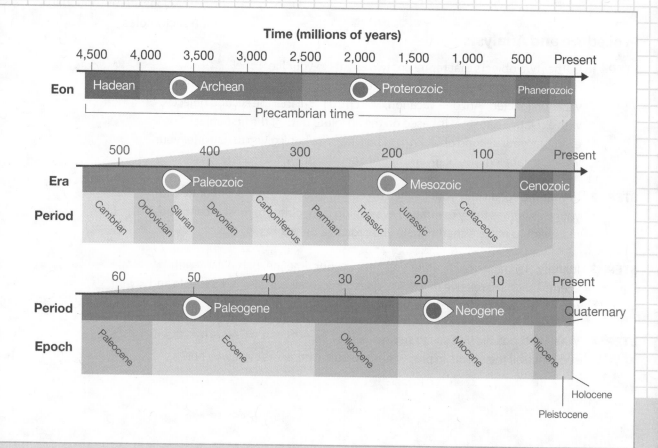

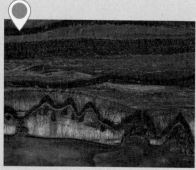

Over 3 billion years ago, photosynthetic organisms released oxygen into Earth's shallow iron-rich seas. Scientists think that oxygen combined with iron to form the red bands in this rock.

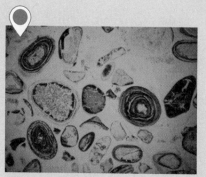

These photosynthetic sea creatures are about 2 billion years old. After all the iron in the seas was used up to form rock, oxygen released by these organisms was added to the air.

Crinoids are animals that flourished during the Paleozoic. These creatures lived anchored to the ocean floor. There are some species of crinoids that still exist today.

Divisions in Geologic Time

The geologic time scale is broken up into the following divisions of time: eons, eras, periods, and epochs. Divisions in the geologic time scale are not equal. This is because the divisions are based on major events and changes in Earth's history, such as extinctions.

Look at the clock-shaped diagram of geologic time. If Earth's history were squeezed into 12 hours, Precambrian time would take up most of that time. Precambrian time began around the time Earth formed and lasted for about 4 billion years. That is almost 90 percent of Earth's 4.6-billion-year history!

 12. Language SmArts How do divisions in the geologic time scale differ from the way we organize time using a clock or a calendar? What is the reason for these differences?

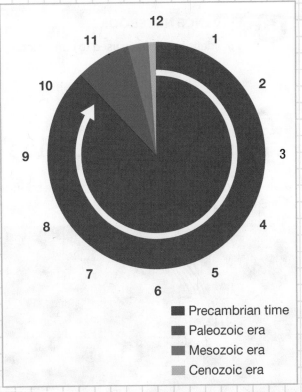

Legend:
- Precambrian time
- Paleozoic era
- Mesozoic era
- Cenozoic era

If all of Earth's history were squeezed into one 12-hour period, Precambrian time would end at about 10:30.

Pterodactylus was a flying meat-eating reptile. It lived during the Jurassic alongside dinosaurs. The fossil record shows that both animals went extinct at the end of the Cretaceous period.

This fossil is of a horse-like mammal from the Paleogene period. During this time, mammals diversified, leading scientists to call this the "Age of Mammals." The first marine mammals also appeared during this time.

This skull is from one of the earliest members of the genus *Homo*. Modern humans, or *Homo sapiens*, evolved about 200,000 years ago.

13. Identify evidence used to construct the geologic time scale.

Language SmArts

Explain Evidence

Fossils and rocks found around the world give scientists clues and provide evidence of what Earth was like in the past.

This fossil is a trilobite, a species that once roamed Earth's oceans. Trilobites went extinct about 250 million years ago.

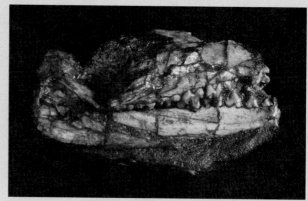

This shows one of the earliest mammals to appear in the fossil record. Mammals appeared about 240 million years ago.

This is Putorana Plateau in Siberia. The plateau formed from a series of volcanic eruptions about 250 million years ago, which may have contributed to the extinction of most life on Earth.

14. In your own words, describe how these fossils and rocks could be used as evidence to construct an explanation for an event that changed life on Earth.

_____

_____

_____

_____

_____

_____

Continue Your Exploration

Name: _____ **Date:** _____

Check out the path below or go online to choose one of the other paths shown.

Careers in Science

- **Hands-On Labs** ✋
- **Exploring the Great Dying**
- **Propose Your Own Path**

Go online to choose one of these other paths.

Paleoartist

If you have ever seen a reconstruction of a dinosaur skeleton at a museum, you know how impressive these ancient creatures are. From rocks, fossils, and reconstructed skeletons, scientists can tell certain things about an extinct animal's appearance, how it moved, and where it lived. For example, fossil footprints can show how an animal walked. The rock that a fossil is found in gives clues about the past environment. For example, coal forms from decaying plants in swamps.

Welcome to the world of paleoart, a profession that combines art and science. Paleoartists help us visualize extinct animals and their environments by creating art, including drawings, three-dimensional models, and digital images. Paleoartists work closely with scientists to make their art as accurate as possible—some paleoartists are even scientists themselves.

This is paleoart of a *Gigantoraptor* on its nest by artist Mohamad Haghani. This dinosaur lived during the Cretaceous period.

Continue Your Exploration

A scientist exploring in the desert found fossil bones of a sheep-sized dinosaur. The bones were reconstructed as shown in this photo. Analysis of the fossil confirmed that the dinosaur was a land reptile that walked on four legs. It had a beak and jaw designed for eating plants. The fossil was found in a sandstone layer that was deposited along the shoreline of a shallow sea. The same sandstone rock in the area contained fossils of ferns and trees.

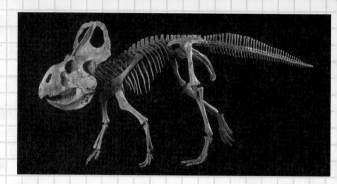

1. What evidence describes this dinosaur and its past environment?

2. **Draw** Use the evidence and the photo to help you draw the dinosaur in its past environment.

3. Fossil evidence does not tell paleoartists everything. For example, the color and skin texture of ancient animals are often unknown. However, paleoartists read scientific papers and study related animals alive today to make inferences about these things. What aspects of your drawing are based on inferences (are not based on direct evidence)?

4. **Collaborate** Compare your paleoart with a classmate. Discuss why there might be differences between your paleoart and your classmate's paleoart.

Can You Explain It?

Name: _____ Date: _____

Revisit the timeline from the beginning of the lesson.

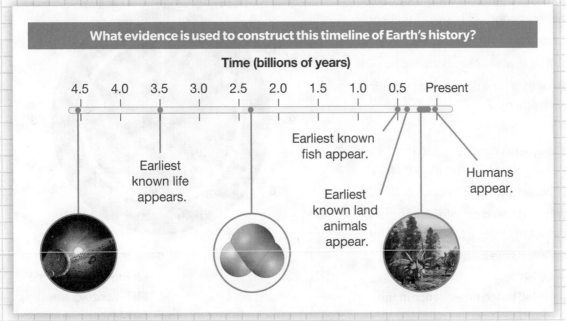

What evidence is used to construct this timeline of Earth's history?

Time (billions of years)

4.5 4.0 3.5 3.0 2.5 2.0 1.5 1.0 0.5 Present

Earliest known life appears.

Earliest known fish appear.

Earliest known land animals appear.

Humans appear.

EVIDENCE NOTEBOOK

Refer to the notes in your Evidence Notebook to help you explain what kinds of evidence are used to construct geologic timelines.

1. State your claim. Make sure your claim fully explains what evidence is used to construct timelines of Earth's history.

2. Summarize the evidence you have gathered to support your claim and explain your reasoning.

Checkpoints

Answer the following questions to check your understanding of the lesson.

Use the diagram to answer Question 3.

3. What does this diagram tell you about these different time periods? Choose all that apply.

   A. the actual length of time for each one

   B. the order in which they occurred

   C. the length of time they lasted in relation to each other

4. Which statements correctly describe the geologic time scale? Choose all that apply.

   A. It is divided into equal periods of time.

   B. It is divided based on evidence in the fossil record.

   C. Some events are arranged according to relative dates.

   D. It is divided based on evidence in the rock record.

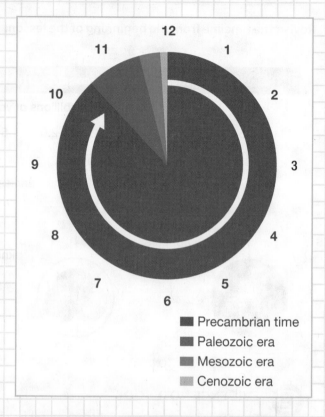

■ Precambrian time
■ Paleozoic era
■ Mesozoic era
■ Cenozoic era

Use the photo to answer Questions 5 and 6.

5. The rock layers in this photo appear undisturbed. Therefore, you can conclude that the white layer is *older / younger* than the red layer, and that the thick brown layer is the *oldest / youngest* of the layers shown here.

6. What is most likely true about these cliffs? Choose all that apply.

   A. They formed over many human lifetimes.

   B. They are formed out of the same kind of rock.

   C. The weathering of these cliffs is a fast geologic process.

   D. Their formation was a slow geologic process.

Interactive Review

Complete this section to review the main concepts of the lesson.

Scientists study current geologic processes to learn about past processes such as tectonic plate motion, weathering, erosion, and deposition.

A. How is it possible to look at geologic processes that shape Earth today to learn about the past?

Scientists use the rock record and the fossil record as evidence for events and conditions in Earth's past.

B. What can you infer from the rock record and the fossil record?

The geologic time scale is used to organize Earth's long history.

C. Why do you think scientists need to organize Earth's history into a time scale?

Choose one of the activities below to explore how this unit connects to other topics.

☐ Computer Science Connection

Re-creating Dinosaurs Using 3D Technology
Advancements in computer animated three-dimensional (3D) technology allow paleontologists to create replicas of dinosaur bones, or fill in missing bones of a partial skeleton fossil. This technology allows scientists to test hypotheses about how dinosaurs and other prehistoric animals moved and lived in their environment.

Using library or Internet resources, research how paleontologists use advancements in 3D scanners and printers to learn more from fossils. Present your findings to the class.

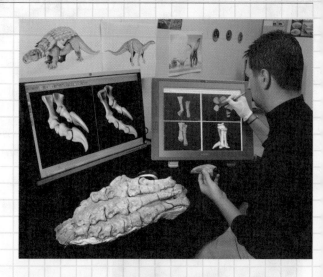

☐ Literature Connection

Dinosaurs in Fictional Literature The scientific discovery and study of dinosaurs has inspired books, movie scripts, and other forms of literature. Some writers base their work on scientific analysis and evidence. Other writers introduce their own ideas, using their imaginations to write about the life and times of dinosaurs.

Select a fictional book or movie that features dinosaurs. Research what scientists know about dinosaur anatomy based on fossil evidence. Write an explanatory essay that describes which aspects of the piece are based on scientific evidence, and which aspects are fictional.

☐ Tools and Technology Connection

Fossil Digging Technology Paleontologists use a variety of tools to help them unearth fossils. Each tool is designed for a specific purpose, whether it is to chisel away rock, brush off sediments, or sift through tiny particles of rock.

Using library or Internet resources, research five different tools that paleontologists may use during a fossil dig. Compare and contrast the structure and function of these tools. Then create an illustrated guide that describes the stages of fossil excavation, including a description of the tools used at each stage.

Name: _____   Date: _____

Complete this review to check your understanding of the unit.

Use the diagram of rock layers to answer Question 1.

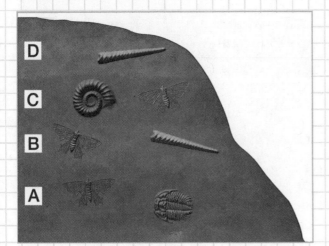

1. Which layer in this diagram is the oldest?

   A. layer A

   B. layer B

   C. layer C

   D. layer D

2. Which of the following do scientists use to help construct a timeline of Earth's history? Select all that apply.

   A. absolute dating

   B. relative dating

   C. rock record

   D. fossil record

3. In which type of rock are fossils most commonly found?

   A. igneous rock

   B. metamorphic rock

   C. sedimentary rock

Use the two images to answer Question 4.

4. The marine animal fossils shown here were found high above sea level in the Himalaya Mountains, shown below. What does this fossil evidence tell us about the past environment of this area?

   A. Many earthquakes occurred in this region.

   B. Volcanoes have erupted in this location.

   C. These rock layers formed when the area was covered by ocean water.

   D. The environment in this area was much colder in the past than it is now.

5. Geologists use the process of
   absolute / relative dating to determine
   the exact age of rocks in years.

Name:

Date:

6. Complete the table by providing at least one example of how each type of evidence relates to each big concept.

Evidence	Patterns	Time and Spatial Scales	Stability and Change
Index fossils			
Relative age of rock layers			
Absolute age of rock layers			

Use the timeline to answer Questions 7–10.

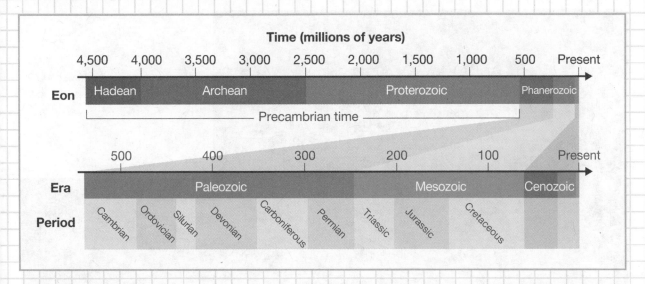

7. How much time is represented by the top part of the timeline? What is the significance of that number?

8. How much time is represented by the bottom portion of the timeline? Explain how the top portion of the timeline relates to the bottom portion.

9. Are the divisions shown by the labeled eons, eras, and periods equal in length? Explain why or why not.

10. Describe the types of evidence that scientists use to construct and update this timeline. What methods do scientists use to supply this evidence?

Use the photo to answer Questions 11–13.

The photo shows the fossil remains of *Tiktaalik* alongside a replica of *Tiktaalik*, which was created based on the fossil. The fossil was discovered on Ellesmere Island in Canada, shown on the map.

11. Describe how this *Tiktaalik* fossil may have formed.

12. Ellesmere Island has an arctic climate. *Tiktaalik* is closely related to an alligator, which lives in warm climates. Based on the location where the *Tiktaalik* fossil was found, describe the climate of Canada at the time the *Tiktaalik* lived. Use evidence to explain your reasoning.

13. Based on the environment in which alligators live and the features of the *Tiktaalik* fossil, describe the environment of Ellesmere Island at the time the *Tiktaalik* lived. Use evidence to explain your reasoning.

Name: _____   Date: _____

How did marine fossils end up in the desert?

Imagine that your group was hiking at the Grand Canyon in Arizona and you discovered a fossil of a cephalopod embedded within limestone rock. You asked the tour guide about the fossil and learned that a cephalopod was a marine organism that is closely related to a squid. You began to wonder how a marine fossil ended up in the dry, hot desert region. You decided to learn more about this fossil and the environment in which this organism thrived. In order to do this, you need to research the area and its geologic history. Collaborate with your group to construct an explanation of how the cephalopod fossil ended up in the Arizona desert.

Cephalopod fossil

The Grand Canyon in Arizona

The steps below will help guide your research and construct your explanation.

1. **Define the Problem** Investigate to learn more about cephalopods and other marine fossils found in the Arizona desert. Define the problem your team is trying to solve.

2. **Conduct Research** Do research to identify the rock layers in the Grand Canyon and the types of fossils found in each layers.

3. **Analyze Data** What is the name of the rock layer in which cephalopod fossils are commonly found? What type of rock is this layer? Explain your answer.

4. **Interpret Data** Using the data you collected in Steps 1–3, what can you infer about the past environments of this area? Describe any events in Earth's history or geological processes that may have contributed to the changing environment.

5. **Construct an Explanation** What is the age of the cephalopod fossil you found? What was the environment like in the area at that time? Provide evidence to support your claim.

✓ **Self-Check**

		I identified the rock layer and type of rock in which the fossil was found.
		I researched how geological processes could have contributed to the Grand Canyon's past environments.
		I analyzed data to estimate an age of the cephalopod fossil.
		I provided evidence to identify the environment of the cephalopod.

Glossary

Sound	Symbol	Example	Respelling	Sound	Symbol	Example	Respelling
				Pronunciation Key			
ă	a	pat	PAT	ŏ	ah	bottle	BAHT'l
ā	ay	pay	PAY	ō	oh	toe	TOH
âr	air	care	KAIR	ô	aw	caught	KAWT
ä	ah	father	FAH•ther	ôr	ohr	roar	ROHR
är	ar	argue	AR•gyoo	oi	oy	noisy	NOYZ•ee
ch	ch	chase	CHAYS	ŏŏ	u	book	BUK
ě	e	pet	PET	ōō	oo	boot	BOOT
ě (at end of a syllable)	eh	settee lessee	seh•TEE leh•SEE	ou	ow	pound	POWND
ěr	ehr	merry	MEHR•ee	s	s	center	SEN•ter
ē	ee	beach	BEECH	sh	sh	cache	CASH
g	g	gas	GAS	ŭ	uh	flood	FLUHD
ĭ	i	pit	PIT	ûr	er	bird	BERD
ĭ (at end of a syllable)	ih	guitar	gih•TAR	z	z	xylophone	ZY•luh•fohn
ī	y eye (only for a complete syllable)	pie island	PY EYE•luhnd	z	z	bags	BAGZ
îr	ir	hear	HIR	zh	zh	decision	dih•SIZH•uhn
j	j	germ	JERM	ə	uh	around broken focus	uh•ROWND BROH•kuhn FOH•kuhs
k	k	kick	KIK	ər	er	winner	WIN•er
ng	ng	thing	THING	th	th	thin they	THIN THAY
ngk	ngk	bank	BANGK	w	w	one	WUHN
				wh	hw	whether	HWETH•er

absolute dating (AB•suh•loot DAYT•ing)
any method of measuring the age of an event or object in years (106)
datación absoluta cualquier método que sirve para determinar la edad de un suceso u objeto en años

convection current (kuhn•VEK•shuhn KER•uhnt)
any movement of matter that results from differences in density; may be vertical, circular, or cyclical (62)
corriente de convección cualquier movimiento de la materia que se produce como resultado de diferencias en la densidad; puede ser vertical, circular o cíclico

deposition (dep•uh•ZISH•uhn)
the process in which material is laid down (10)
sublimación inversa el proceso por medio del cual un material se deposita

Earth system (ERTH SIS•tuhm)
all of the nonliving things, living things, and processes that make up the planet Earth, including the geosphere, the hydrosphere, the atmosphere, and the biosphere (70)
sistema terrestre todos los seres vivos y no vivos y todos los procesos que conforman el planeta Tierra, incluidas la geósfera, la hidrósfera, la atmosfera y la biósfera

erosion (ee•ROH•zhuhn)
the process by which wind, water, ice, or gravity transports soil and sediment from one location to another (10)
erosión el proceso por medio del cual el viento, el agua, el hielo o la gravedad transporta tierra y sedimentos de un lugar a otro

geologic time scale (jee•uh•LAHJ•ik TYM SKAYL)
the standard method used to divide Earth's long natural history into manageable parts (122)
escala de tiempo geológico el método estándar que se usa para dividir la larga historia natural de la Tierra en partes razonables

igneous rock (IG•nee•uhs RAHK)
rock that forms when magma cools and solidifies (26)
roca ígnea una roca que se forma cuando el magma se enfría y se solidifica

metamorphic rock (met•uh•MOHR•fik RAHK)
a rock that forms from other rocks as a result of intense heat, pressure, or chemical processes (34)
roca metamórfica una roca que se forma a partir de otras rocas como resultado de calor intenso, presión o procesos químicos

mineral (MIN•er•uhl)
a natural, usually inorganic solid that has a characteristic chemical composition and an orderly internal structure (24)
mineral un sólido natural, normalmente inorgánico, que tiene una composición química característica y una estructura interna ordenada

plate tectonics (PLAYT tek•TAHN•iks)
the theory that explains how large pieces of Earth's outermost layer, called tectonic plates, move and change shape (61)
tectónica de placas la teoría que explica cómo se mueven y cambian de forma las placas tectónicas, que son grandes porciones de la capa más externa de la Tierra

relative dating (REL•uh•tiv DAYT•ing)
any method of determining whether an event or object is older or younger than other events or objects (104)
datación relativa cualquier método que se utiliza para determinar si un acontecimiento u objeto es más viejo o más joven que otros acontecimientos u objetos

sediment (SED•uh•muhnt)
fragments of organic or inorganic material that are transported and deposited by wind, water, or ice and that accumulate in layers on Earth's surface (6)
sedimento fragmentos de material orgánico o inorgánico que son transportados y depositados por el viento, agua o hielo y que se acumulan en capas en la superficie de la Tierra

sedimentary rock (sed•uh•MEN•tuh•ree RAHK)
a rock that forms from compressed or cemented layers of sediment (30)
roca sedimentaria una roca que se forma a partir de capas comprimidas o cementadas de sedimento

tectonic plate (tek•TAHN•ik PLAYT)
a block of lithosphere that consists of the crust and the rigid, outermost part of the mantle (56)
placa tectónica un bloque de litosfera formado por la corteza y la parte rígida y más externa del manto

weathering (WETH•er•ing)
the natural process by which atmospheric and environmental agents, such as wind, rain, and temperature changes, disintegrate and decompose rocks (6)
meteorización el proceso natural por medio del cual los agentes atmosféricos o ambientales, como el viento, la lluvia y los cambios de temperatura, desintegran y descomponen las rocas

Index

Page numbers for key terms are in **boldface** type.
Page numbers in *italic* type indicate illustrative material, such as photographs, graphs, charts and maps.

A

abrasion, 7, *7*, 10, 11, *11*
absolute age, 106
    determining, 107
    of Earth, 108
    using, 106–108
absolute dating, 106, 118
acid precipitation, 8, *8*, 16
Age of Mammals, 125
air, weathering of rock, 8, *8*
Alaska, volcanic eruptions on
        islands, 61, *61*
Aleutian Trench, 66, *66*
alluvial fan, 20, 74, *74*
amber fossil, 122, *122*
amphibolite, 35, *35*
analysis
    of effects of weathering, 9, *9*, 92
    of erosion and deposition, 15
    of fossils to describe Earth's past,
        100
    of model of crystal formation, 27
    of movement of continents, 58–59
    of rock formation, 103
    of rock layers, 119–120
    of time scales, 123
    of visual evidence, 78–79
animals
    fossils of, 99, *99*, 100, 109
    weathering of rock, 7
Antarctica, fossil from, *49*
Appalachian Mountains, 36, *50*
approximation
    of age of rocks, 33
Arches National Park, Utah, 22, *22*
argon, 71
Art Connection
    Geology and Society, 86
ash, 78, *78*
Ashfall Fossil Beds, *109*, 109–110
Assessment
    Lesson Self-Check, 19–21, 43–45,

65–67, 83–85, 111–113, 129–131
    Unit Performance Task, 91–92,
        137–138
    Unit Review, 87–90, 133–136
Atlantic Ocean, 76
Atlas Mountains, *50*
atmosphere, *71*, 71–73, 85

B

Banff National Park, Alberta,
        Canada, 68, *68*
Barringer Meteorite Crater, 69, *69*,
        83, *83*
basalt, 28, *28*, 35, *35*, 98, 119, *119*
biosphere, *71*, 71–73, 85
blueschist, 36
boundaries of tectonic plates,
        56–57, *57*, 60, 61
breccia, 30, *30*
bridge design, 91–92
brittle star, *105*, 120, *120*, *131*

C

calcite, 30
calcium carbonate, 30, 31, 32, 33
calculation
    rate of change on Earth's surface,
        76, *76*
    rate of erosion, 10
    rate of sea-floor Spreading, 54
caldera, 81
Can You Explain It? 5, 19, 23, 43, 47,
        65, 69, 83, 97, 111, 115, 129
carbon dioxide, 71
Careers in Science, 127–128
Cascade Range, 78, *78*
caves
    crystal formation in, 24, *24*, 32
    formation of, 8
    stalactite formation in, 24, 32
cementation, 32, 39, *39*

Cenozoic era, 125, *125*
cephalopod, 137
change
    in crust of Earth, 46–62, 68–82,
        84–85, *84*, *85*
    to Earth's surface, *74*, *76*, *77*, *78*, *79*,
        80, 74–80,
        geologic change, 5–18, 116, *116*,
        117
    half-life of radioactive elements,
        107, *107*
    of life forms, 97, 119, *119*, 122, *122*,
        124, *124*, 125, *125*
    in rocks, 22–42, *38*, *39*, *45*, 98, *98*
    weathering, erosion, and deposition
        of rock, 5, 6, 6–18, 7, 8, 9, 11, 12,
        13, 14, 16
    in Yellowstone National Park, 81,
        81–82, 82
Checkpoints, 20, 44, 66, 84, 112, 130
chemical weathering, 6, 8, *8*, 9, 21,
        21, 74, *74*
climate, 8, 29
coal, *119*
    formation of, 30, 41, *41*, 102
    mining of, 41–42
coarse-grained igneous rock, 28, *28*
Collaborate, 18, 42, 64, 82, 110, 128
Colorado River, 1, *1*, 23, *23*, 32, 117,
        117
Communicate, 92
compaction, 32, *39*
components of Earth's system, 71,
        71–72, 85
Computer Science Connection
    Re-creating Dinosaurs Using 3D
        Technology, 132
computer simulation, 14
conglomerate rocks, 119, *119*
conservation of matter, 10
continental shelves, 50, *50*, 51, *51*, 52
continents
    model of movement of, 58–59
    movement of, 48, *48*, 59, *59*

contour maps, *76, 78, 79*
convection currents, 62, *62, 67, 67*
copper, *41*
core of Earth, *70, 73*
Correlate Rock Sequences, *121*
crocodiles, *120*
crystals
    formation of, *24, 24, 32*
    in igneous rock, *28, 28*
    modeling formation of, *27*
    in sedimentary rock, *30*
currents, 62, *62*
cycle
    of energy, *72, 72–73, 73*
    of material in oceans, *55*
    of matter in Earth's interior, *62, 62, 73, 73*
    of plate tectonics, *62, 62*
    of rock formation and destruction, *22–42, 38, 39, 45*
    of weathering, *7–8*
Cynognathus, *48, 48, 66*

D

dams, *14, 14*
data
    on earthquakes, *63, 63*
    fossil evidence, *48, 48–49, 49, 67, 67*
    landform data, *50, 50–51*
    oceanic data, *52, 52–55, 53, 54, 55*
deep-ocean trenches, *52, 52, 55*
    formation of, *55, 56, 57, 57, 66, 66, 74*
delta, *11, 11, 77, 77, 87*
deposition, 4, 10–13, *74, 98*
    changing Earth's surface, *74, 74, 75*
    cycling matter, *72*
    of gold in veins and nuggets, *17*
    modeling, *14–16, 14*
    river delta formation, *11, 11, 77, 77, 87, 87*
    in rock cycle, *39, 39*
    sedimentary rock formation, *25, 25, 32, 99*
    time scale of, *16, 21, 75*
Devil's Tower, Wyoming, *29, 29*

diagram, *13, 18, 39, 45, 52, 53, 57, 62, 64, 67, 73, 90, 91, 91, 103, 105, 112, 121, 124, 125, 129, 130*
difference
    in continental shapes, *59, 59*
    between Earth and moon's systems, *70, 70*
    in rock formations, *33, 33*
    in weathering, *6*
Dinosaur Provincial Park, *97*
dinosaurs, *97, 97, 111, 114, 125, 125, 127, 128, 132*
diorite, *28*
Discuss, *9, 11, 16, 25, 26, 32, 34, 37, 39, 48, 53, 73, 74, 98, 102, 106, 116*
Do the Math
    Buried in Time, *31*
    Calculate Rate of Erosion, *10*
    Calculate the Rate of Change on Earth's Surface, *76*
    Calculate the Rate of Sea-Floor Spreading, *54*
    Describe Scales of Time, *117*
    Determine Absolute Age, *107*
Draw, *16, 40, 47, 103, 122, 128*

E

Earth
    absolute age of, *108*
    changing surface of, *1, 68–82, 104–105, 115*
    energy from the interior of, *73, 73*
    history of, *93, 114–128, 129, 129*
    rock cycle on, *22–42, 98*
    subsystems of, *71, 71–73, 72, 73, 85*
    tectonic plates of, *46–64*
    timeline, *95*
    weathering, erosion, and deposition on, *5–18*
earthquakes, *103*
    causes of, *60, 63, 73*
    changes in rocks, *40*
    changes to Earth's surface, *74, 76, 78*
    high-risk area, *64*
    on ocean floor, *53, 55*

    at plate boundaries, *57, 57, 60, 64*
    warning system, *63, 63–64*
    in Yellowstone National Park, *81*
earthquake warning system, *63, 63–64*
Earth's subsystems, *71, 71–72*
Earth's surface
    changes in, *74–77, 114–117*
    modeling, *56–57*
    time scale of changes, *75, 80, 85*
Earth system, 70, *70*
    cycling of matter and energy in, *72, 72*
    metamorphic rocks in, *34–37*
    subsystems of, *71, 71–73, 72, 73, 85*
electricity generation, *41*
energy
    in coal, *41*
    cycle of, *72, 72–73, 73*
    of Earth's interior, *62, 73, 73, 81*
    of Earth's system, *70, 85*
    from the sun, *12*
    transfer through Earth system, *85*
    in volcanic eruptions, *73*
    for weathering, *10, 12, 13*
Engineering Connection
    Seeing the Unseen Through Data, *86*
Engineer It, *14, 31, 61, 76, 99, 123*
    Performance Task, *91–92, 137–138*
environment, fossil evidence in, *100*
eons, *125*
epochs, *125*
equation for rate of spreading, *54*
eras, *125*
erosion, 4, 9–13, 10, *19, 19, 21, 21*
    alluvial fan formation, *74*
    changes to Earth's surface, *74, 75, 98, 116*
    cycling matter, *72*
    by glaciers, *29, 37, 37*
    of gold particles, *17*
    modeling, *14–16, 14*
    river delta formation, *11, 11*
    in rock cycle, *39, 39*
    sedimentary rock formation, *99, 105*
    time scale of, *16, 21, 75*

evaporation

formation of sedimentary rock, 30

mineral formation, 24

evidence

in fossils, 97, 97, 104–105, 105, 122, 122, 124, 124

of plate tectonics, 48, 48–56, 49, 50, 52, 54, 55, 61, 62, 67, 67

of a process, 118

in rock and fossil records, 97, 97, 104, 104–105, 105, 122, 124, 124

in rock formations, 98, 118

Evidence Notebook, 5, 8, 13, 19, 23, 25, 33, 39, 43, 47, 55, 56, 59, 61, 65, 69, 71, 75, 77, 83, 97, 104, 108, 111, 115, 119, 126, 129

explanation

of age of ocean floor, 55

of changes on Earth's surface, 74–77

of Earth's system interactions, 73

of observations of evidence of tectonic plates, 51

of plate motion, 60–62

Exploration

Analyzing Continental Data, 48–51

Analyzing Interactions Within the Earth System, 70–73

Analyzing Oceanic Data, 52–55

Comparing Minerals and Rocks, 24–25

Describing Evidence for the Geologic Time Scale, 122–126

Describing Geologic Change, 116–117

Describing the Formation of Sedimentary Rocks and Fossils, 98–100

Determining the Relative Ages of Rocks, 101–105

Explaining Evidence of Earth's Past, 118–121

Explaining Plate Motion, 60–62

Explaining the Changes on Earth's Surface, 74–77

Exploring Agents of Erosion and Deposition, 10–13

Identifying Effects of Weathering, 6–9

Modeling Earth's Surface, 56–57

Modeling the Rock Cycle, 38–40

Modeling Weathering, Erosion, and Deposition, 14, 14–16

Relating Igneous Rocks to the Earth System, 26–29

Relating Metamorphic Rocks to the Earth System, 34–37

Relating Sedimentary Rocks to the Earth System, 30–33

Using Absolute and Relative Age, 106–108

Explore ONLINE!, 10, 26, 31, 47, 59, 60, 65, 72, 73

extinction, 116, 126

of dinosaurs, 125, 125

extrusive igneous rock, 26, 28, 29, 29

F

fault, 81, 103, 104, 105, 112

fine-grained igneous rock, 28, 28

floods, 14, 14

changes in rocks, 40

changes to Earth's surface, 75, 77, 77

flow of energy and matter, 26

fog, 71

forest fire, 73, 73

formula for rate of spreading, 54

fossil

evidence of life in past, 49, 49, 66

evidence of tectonic plates, 48, 48, 61, 67, 67

preservation of, 49

sedimentary rock formation, 30

types of, 49, 49

fossil record, 104, 119, 122

fossils, 100, 105, 113, 114, 120, 125, 131, 133

age determination, 97

aging of, 119

in Ashfall Fossil Beds, 109

in desert, 137

digging technology for recovery, 132

evidence of Earth's changes in, 100–101, 104, 118, 119, 131, 131

evidence of life on Earth, 122, 122, 124, 124, 125, 125–126, 126

formation of, 99, 99–100, 100, 109

relative dating of, 104

G

geologic change, 116, 116, 117, 117

rate of, 116

tectonic plate movement, 46, 46, 56, 56–57, 59, 59, 73, 74, 74, 76, 76

time scale, 116

weathering, erosion, and deposition, 5–18

geologic features, 1, 3, 86, 96, 116

geologic processes

changing Earth's surface, 74–77, 85, 116, 116–117

igneous rock formation, 26, 26

metamorphic rock formation, 34, 34

in rock cycle, 26, 38, 38, 39, 45

sedimentary rock formation, 31, 30–31

geologic time scale, 122–128, 124, 131

divisions in, 125, 125

geosphere

elements of, 71, 71, 72, 73, 85

igneous rock in, 28

metamorphic rock in, 36, 36

sedimentary rock in, 32

geyser, 81, 81–82

Gibbons, Doug, 63, 63–64

Glacial Lake Missoula, 14, 14

glaciers

erosion and deposition by, 12, 12, 20, 20, 29, 37, 37, 116, 116

Missoula Floods and, 14, 14

movement of, 76, 77

Global Positioning System (GPS), 61

Glossopteris, 48, 48, 66

gneiss, 34, 34, 36, 36

gold, search for, 18, 17–18

GPS (Global Positioning System), 61

Grand Canyon, Arizona, 1, 23, 23, 33, 43, 43, 117, 137

granite, 41
  formation of, 28, *28*, 98
  resistance to weathering, 6
gravel, 41
gravity
  erosion and deposition by, 10, 12, *12*, 21
  rain, 72
  role in convection currents, 62
  weathering of rock, 7, *7*, 8
Great Lakes, 12
greenschist, 36, *36*
groundwater, 8
gypsum, 24, *24*, 41, 99

H

Half Dome, Yosemite National Park, 29, *29*
half-life, 107
Hands-On Lab
  Analyze Visual Evidence, 78–79
  Construct a Time Scale, 123–124
  Model Crystal Formation, 27
  Model Erosion and Deposition, 15–16
  Model Rock Layers to Determine Relative Age, 102–103
  Model the Movement of Continents, 58–59
heat
  rock cycle, *39, 45, 90*
Himalayas, 60, *60*, 74, 117
history of Earth, 114–128
Holocene epoch, 124, *124*
hornfels, 34, *34*
hot springs, 81
humans
  actions changing rocks, 40
  earliest fossil of, 125, *125*
hydrosphere, 71, *71*, 72, 73, 85
hydrothermal features, 81, *81*

I–K

ice
  erosion and deposition by, 10, 12, *12*, 21, 75
  fossils in, 99
  weathering of rock, 6, 7, *7*, 16
Identify Areas of Erosion and Deposition, 13, *13*
Identify How Sedimentary Rock Forms and Changes, 33
igneous intrusion, *103*, 104
igneous rock, *25*, **26,** *26, 29, 45*, 119, *119*, 120, *120*
  absolute dating of, 106, 108
  coarse-grained and fine-grained, 28, *28*
  formation of, 39, *39*, 98, 107, *107*, 120, *120*
  fossil formation in, 109
  in geosphere, 28
  intrusive and extrusive, 26, 28, 29, *29*
  metamorphic rock formation, 34–35
  time scale for formation of, 28
  weathering of, 29, *29*
index fossil, 104, 105, *105*, 126
infer, 73, 105, 128
interactions of Earth's subsystems, 71–73, *72, 73*, 80
Interactive Review, 21, 45, 67, 85, 113, 131
intrusive igneous rock, 26, 28, 29, *29*
iron, 41
island formation, 47, *47*, 56, 57, 61, 65, *65*

L

landform
  evidence of tectonic plates, 48, *48*, 50, *50*, 51, 61
landslide, 12, *12*, 84, *84*, 117, *117*
Language SmArts, 103, 110, 125
  Analyze the Effects of Weathering, 9
  Cite Evidence for Plate Tectonics, 62
  Examine Changes over Time, 80
  Explain Evidence, 126
  Model the Rock Cycle, 40
lava, 60
  cycling of energy and matter, 73, *73*
  flow, *26*, 103, *103*
  formation of igneous rocks, 98

formation of rock, 25, *25*, 26, *26*, 28, 29, *29*, 119, *119*
  mineral formation, 24
lead, 107, *107*
Lesson Self-Check, 19–21, 43–45, 65–67, 83–85, 111–113, 129–131
lichen, 8, *8*, 74
limestone, 30, 32, *32*, 33, *33*, 37, *38*, 41
  formation of, 98, 99, 102
linear sea, 53, *53*
Literature Connection
  Dinosaurs in Fictional Literature, 132
location, effect on weathering, 8
Lystrosaurus, 48, *48*, 66

M

magma
  cycling of energy and matter, 73, *73*
  formation of, 25
  formation of igneous rocks, 98
  formation of rock, 25, *25*, 26, *26*, 29, *29*
  igneous rocks formation, 28
  metamorphic rock formation, 34, *34*, 35
  mineral formation, 24
  sea-floor spreading and, 53
  volcanic mountain chains formed by, 55, 57, *57*
  volcano formation, 60, *60*
  Yellowstone volcano eruption, 81–82
magma chamber, 34, *34*, 35, 73, 81
mammals, *125*, 126
mantle, 73, *73*, 74
marble, 37, *37*, *38*, 41
mass extinction, 116
matter
  conservation of, 6, 10
  cycle of, 55, 72, *72*
  recycled in rock cycle, 38
  transfer through Earth system, 85
melting, *39, 45, 90*, 98
Mesa Verde Canyon, Arizona, 16, *16*
Mesosaurus, 48, *48*, 49, *49*, 66

Mesozoic era, 124, *124,* 125, *130*
metamorphic rock, *45*
  formation of, *34,* 34–37, *35, 37,* 39, *39, 77*
  in geosphere, 36, *36*
  time scale for formation of, 36
metamorphosis, 34, 35, *35*
meteorites, 69, *69,* 75, 83, *83,* 108, 116
methods
  absolute dating of rock, 106, 118
  relative dating of rock, 104–105, 118
mica, 35, *35*
Mid-Atlantic Ridge, 52, *52,* 54, *54,* 76, *76*
mid-ocean ridges
  discovery of, 52, *52*
  formation of, *53,* 53–54, 67, *67,* 76, *76*
  map of, *55*
  plate tectonics explaining, 61
  widening of ocean basin, 57, *57*
minerals, 24
  change of, 34
  dissolved in water, 32
  in igneous rock, 26
  mining of, 41
  as part of geosphere, 71
  resistance to weathering, 6
  rocks compared to, 24–25
  sedimentary rock formation, 30
  volcanic eruption of, 73, *73*
mining, 41–42
Missoula Floods, 14, *14*
model/modeling
  crystal formation, 27
  of Earth's surface, *56,* 56–57
  function of, 61
  movement of continents, 58–59
  rock cycle, 38–40
  rock layers, 102–103
  weathering, erosion, and deposition, *14,* 14–16
Monument Valley, Arizona, 33, *33*
moon, 70, *70*
moss, 8, *8*

motion/movement of tectonic plates, 46, *46, 56,* 56–57, *57,* 59, *59, 60,* 60–62, *62,* 73, 74, *74,* 76, *76*
mountains
  erosion of, 74
  evidence of tectonic plates, 50, *50*
  formation of, 36, 56, 57, *57,* 60, 68, *68,* 74, 75, 76, 116, 117, *117*
  on ocean floor, 55
Mount St. Helens National Volcanic Monument, 78, *78*
mudstone, 30

N

Neogene period, *124*
North American plate, *61*

O

observations, 15, 27, 44, 48, 49, 51, 58, 59, 79,
obsidian, 28
ocean basins, 56, 74
ocean floor
  age of, 55
  deep-ocean trenches, 52, *52,* 55, *55,* 66, *66,* 74, 76
  mid-ocean ridge, *52,* 52–53, *53,* 55, 76, *76*
  rift valley, *52,* 53, *53*
  sea-floor spreading, *53,* 53–54, 61
oceans
  erosion of shores, 74
  formation of, *53,* 53–54
  as part of hydrosphere, 71
online activities, Explore ONLINE!, 10, 26, 31, 47, 59, 60, 65, 72, 73
Oregon hills, *96*
oxidation, 8, *8,* 74, *74*

P

Pacific Northwest Seismic Network (PNSN), 63
Pacific plate, *61*
paleoartist, *127,* 127–128

Paleogene period, *124*
Paleogeography, 95
Paleozoic era, 93, 124, *124,* 125, *125, 130*
Pangaea, 56, 58, 59, *59*
parts of Earth's system, *71,* 71–74, 85
patterns
  in crystals, 24, *24*
  in fossil locations, 67
  in rocks, 98, *98*
  of half-life, 107, *107*
  of ocean floor, 53, 55, *55,* 56
  of sand dunes, 11, *11*
peat formation, 30
People in Science, 63–64
period, as a division of time, 124, *124,* 125
Permian period, 124, *124*
Phanerozoic eon, 124, *124*
photosynthetic organisms, 124, *124*
phyllite, 35, *35*
Physical Science Connection, Sonar and the Ocean Floor, 86
physical weathering, 6, 7, *7,* 8, 9, *9,* 21, *21*
plants
  break down of rocks, 74, *74*
  fossils of, 99, *100*
  weathering of rock, 7, *7,* 8, *8*
plate boundaries, 56, 57, *57,* 60, *60,* 66
plate motion, 104, *105*
plate tectonics, 61
  causes of plate motion, 62, *62*
  changes due to, *60*
  theory of, 61
PNSN (Pacific Northwest Seismic Network), 63
Port Campbell National Park, Australia, 5, *5,* 19, *19*
Praia do Camilo, Lagos, Portugal, *4*
Precambrian time, 122, 124, *124,* 125, *125, 130*
predictions
  by modeling Earth's surface, 15
  of Earth's changes, 13, 16
  of plate motion, 59
  with computer simulations, 14

pressure
    metamorphic rock formation, 34, *34, 35, 36, 36–37, 37*
    mineral formation, 24
    rock formation, 25, *25,* 39, *39*
    sedimentary rock formation, 30, 39, *39*
    weathering of rock, 7
processes
    disturbance of rock layers, 104
    of Earth's system, 70
    of erosion and deposition, 98
    evidence of Earth's past, 118
    of formation of minerals, 24, *24*
    geologic processes, 26, *26,* 30–31, *31,* 34, *34,* 75, 85, *85,* 116, 131
    oxidation, 8, *8*
    at plate boundaries, 56–57, *57,* 76, *76*
    in rock cycle, 25, *25,* 38, *38, 39*
    sea-floor spreading and mid-ocean ridge formation, 53, *53,* 67, *67*
    uplift, 28, 32, 33, 36
    weathering, erosion, and deposition, 5–16
properties
    of marble, 37
    of minerals, 24
Proterozoic eon, *124*
pumice, 29, *29*
Putorana Plateau, 126, *126*
P-waves, 63–64, *64*
pyroclastic flows, 78

Q

quarry, 41, *41*
quartz, 30
quartzite, 35
Quaternary period, 124, *124*

R

Rainbow Mountains, China, 33, *33*
reasoning, explanation of, 19, 43, 65, 83, 111, 129
relative age, 101, 104–105, 106

relative dating, 104, 118
    of fossils, 104
    of rocks, 104–105
    unconformities and, 105
    using, 106–108
review
    Lesson Self-Check, 19–21, 43–45, 65–67, 83–85, 111–113, 129–131
    Unit, 87–90, 133–136
rift valley, *52,* 53, *53,* 57, *57*
river delta formation, 11, *11, 20,* 77, *77*
rivers, erosion and deposition by, 10, 11, *11,* 77, *77*
rock
    break down of, 74, *74*
    erosion and deposition, 10–16, *11, 13, 14, 16,* 74
    evidence of continental drift, 48, 51
    factors changing, 40
    formation of, 25, *25,* 35, *35,* 98, 98–99, *99*
    igneous rock, 25, **26,** *26,* 28–29, *29,* 34–35, 39, *39, 45*
    metamorphic rock, *34,* **34**–37, *35, 36, 37,* 39, *39, 45,* 77
    minerals compared to, 24–25
    mining of, 41–42
    as part of geosphere, 71
    sedimentary rock, 25, *25,* 30, **30**–35, *31, 32, 33,* 39, *39, 45,* 77
    uses of, 41
    volcanic eruption of, 73, *73*
    weathering of, 5, *6,* 6–9, *7, 8, 9*
rock cycle, 22–32, 38–40, *39, 45,* 90
rock falls, 12
rock record, 104–105, 118, 122
rocks
    analysis of layers, 119, 120
    evidence of Earth's history in, 104, *118,* 118–119, *119*
    formation of, 25, *25,* 35, *35,* 98, 98–99, *99*
    using absolute and relative age, 106–108
rock sequences, 121, *121*
Rocky Mountains, Rockies, 28

S

sand, 41
sand bars, 10, *10*
sand dune, 6, 11, *11,* 16
sandstone, 30, 31, 33, *33,* 35
    formation of, 102
    fossils in, 120, *120*
San Francisco, *3*
Scablands, 14, *14*
scale
    of changes on Earth's surface, 74, *74*
    of weathering, erosion, and deposition, 16
schist, 36, *36*
sea-floor spreading, *53,* 53–54, 61, 76
sediment, 6, 99, *99*
    alluvial fan formation, 74
    cycling matter, 72
    deposition of, *10,* 10–13, *11, 12,* 116
    formation of, 25, 32
    river delta formation, 11, *11,* 77, *77*
    sand dune formation, 6, 11, *11*
    sedimentary rock formation, *30,* 30–31, *31,* 39, *39,* 98–99, *105*
    weathering of rock, 7, *7*
sedimentary rock, 30, *45, 112, 113*
    formation of, 25, *25,* 30, 30–31, *31,* 33, *33,* 39, *39,* 77, 98–100, *105,* 118
    fossil formation in, 99–100
    in geosphere, 32
    layers of, *98, 108*
    metamorphic rock formation, 34–35
    relative dating, 108
    time scale for formation of, 32, *32*
    weathering and erosion of, 33, *33*
seismic waves, 63–64, *64,* 86, *86*
seismogram, *86*
shale, 32, *32,* 34, 35, *35,* 102, 118, 120, *120*
sheep-sized dinosaur, 128, *128*
shells, 33, 38, *38,* 99, *99*
shorelines, 52
siltstone, 98, 102
slate, 34, *34,* 35, *35*

soil, 6

South Coyote Buttes Wilderness, Arizona, 6, *6*

Sphinx, 16, *16*

stalactite, 32, *32,* 76

starfish, *100, 105, 120*

***Starry Night Over the Rhone* (van Gogh),** *86*

St. Helens, Mount, 78, *78–79, 79*

subsystems of Earth, 71, *71–74, 73*

sun

as driver of erosion and deposition, 72

energy from, 12, 13, 41, 72

powering weathering, erosion, deposition, 12, 13

supercontinent, 56

surface area and weathering, 6, 8

surface features, 57, *57*

S-waves, 63–64, *64*

system, Earth, 70

T

tables

of absolute and relative ages, 106

of crystal formation observations, 27

of data on changes on Earth's surface, 76

of data on rock layers and fossils, *110*

of erosion and deposition predictions and observations, *15*

of fossil data observations, *49*

of half-life data, *107*

of landform data observations, *51*

of rock layers, *102*

of statements about Earth and moon, *70*

of types of weathering, *9*

Why It Matters, 2, 94

Take It Further

Careers in Science: Paleoartist, 127–128

Coal Mining, 41–42

Exploring the Ashfall Fossil Beds, 109–110

Gold Rush, 17–18

People in Science: Doug Gibbons 63–64

Yellowstone Is Changing, 81–82, *81*

tar, fossils in, 99

technology

3D imaging, *132*

tectonic plates, 46–64, **56,** *56, 57*

deep-ocean trench formation, 52, *52, 55, 55,* 56, 57, *57,* 66, *66,* 67, *67,* 74, 76

large-scale changes at, 74

mid-ocean ridge formation, 52, *52,* 53, 53–54, 57, *57,* 61, 67, *67,* 76, 76

mountain formation, 36, 57, *57,* 60, 68, *68,* 74, 76

movement of, 46, *46,* 56, 56–57, 59, *59,* 73, 74, *74,* 76, *76,* 116, 131

temperature(s)

metamorphic rock formation, 34, *34,* 35, 36, 36–37, *37*

mineral formation, 24

rock formation, 25, *25,* 39, *39*

sedimentary rock formation, 30, 39, *39*

weathering of rock, 7, 8

See also **heat.**

theory of plate tectonics, 61

time scale

changes to Earth's surface, 75–77, *77,* 80

erosion and deposition, 13, 16, *16,* 21

geologic time scale, **122,** 124, *124*

igneous rock formation, 28

metamorphic rock formation, 36

of rock cycle, 26

sedimentary rock formation, 32, *32*

weathering of rock, 9, 13, 16, *16,* 21

Tools and Technology Connection

Fossil Digging Technology, 132

transfer of energy, 72–73

travertine, 31, *31,* 32

tree sap, fossils in, 99

trilobite, *105, 113*

tuff, 118, *118*

turtle, fossil, *120, 131*

tyrannosaur skeleton, 114, *114*

U

unconformity, 105

underwater canyon, Iceland, 46, *46*

Unit Performance Task

How did marine fossils end up in the desert? 137–138

What is the best location for a new bridge? 91–92

Unit Project

Feature Future, 3

Paleogeography, 95

Unit Starter

Identifying Geologic Features, 3

Sequence of Events, 95

Unit Review, 87–90, 133–136

uplift, 28, 32, 33, 36

uranium, *107*

V

valleys, formation of, 11, *11,* 53, 75, *116*

Vanuatu, 60, *60*

volcanic islands, 47, *47,* 56, 57, 61, 65, *65*

volcanic mountain chains, 55, 56, 57, *57*

volcano

ashfall from, 109

eruption of Mount St. Helens, *78,* 78–80

eruptions of, 56, 57, 60, *60,* 73, *73,* 78, *78–79,* 116, 120, *120, 126*

eruptions on ocean floor, 53, *53*

formation of, 60, *60*

formation of igneous rocks, 26, *26,* 120, *120*

formation of mountains, 126, *126*

island formation, 47, *47,* 56, 57, 61, 65, *65*

trenches on ocean floor, 55

W–X

Wallula Gap, *14*

water

erosion and deposition by, 10–11, *11*, 12, 16, *16*, 21, *21*, 33, *33*, 75

in hydrosphere, 71, *71*

movement of matter, 72

sedimentary rock formation, 32

waterfall, 12, *12*

weathering of rock, 6, 7, *7*, 8, 9, *9*, 29, 33, *33*

waves, erosion and deposition by, 11, *11*

weathering, *4,* **6,** *6,* 19, *19*

agents of, 6–9, 87

changes to Earth's surface, 116, *116,* 131

chemical, 6, 8, *8,* 9, *9,* 21, *21*

of igneous rock, 29, *29*

of metamorphic rock, 37, *37*

modeling, *14,* 14–15

physical, 6–7, *7,* 8, 9, *9,* 21, 21

in rock cycle, 39, *39*

of rock with gold, 17

of sedimentary rock, 33, *33*

sediment formation, 25, *25,* 39, *39,* 74, *74*

time scale of, 16

West Mata volcano, 60, *60*

White Cliffs of Dover, England, 33, *33*

Why It Matters, 2, 94

wind

erosion and deposition by, 10–11, *11,* 12, 21, *21,* 33, 75

weathering of rock, 6, 7, *7,* 9, *9,* 16, *16,* 29, *29,* 33, *33*

Write, 80

Y–Z

Yellowstone caldera, 81–82, *82*

Yellowstone National Park, *81,* 81–82, *82*